"*Twelve Unending Summers* is a remarkable and timely tale of the power of the human spirit. So many things went wrong and right in this remarkable young man's journey. It touches the heart while providing great insight into life in Haiti, the Bahamas, and America for a young man who by all rights should have failed, yet did just the opposite. I am proud to have played a small part in his journey."

David T. Hughes
CEO (retired), Boys and Girls Clubs of Broward County

"Cholet Josué's fascinating autobiography puts flesh on the bones of a story that is often too abstract: the perilous journey that desperate Haitians make to get to America. It is all here, the dangerous boat trip across the Caribbean, the years of living in the shadows as an undocumented immigrant in South Florida, and the part that is far less known: ultimate success in his adopted country. Josué earned a degree in chemistry while still illegal, represented himself successfully in deportation hearings, and went on to complete medical school. This is an engrossing human triumph and a genuine American story."

Joel Dreyfuss, Haitian American journalist and author

"'Kelly' is an extraordinary human being. *Twelve Unending Summers* is an inspiring memoir of a life of humble beginnings and limited resources that dared to dream…creating a tapestry of what his tomorrows could be. It was my privilege to share my space with him as his advisor in medical school and to see him soar. I highly recommend this book to the young and the maturing who dare to dream dreams of their tomorrows."

Professor of Neurobiology, Morehous

# TWELVE UNENDING SUMMERS

## MEMOIR OF AN IMMIGRANT CHILD

# Twelve Unending Summers

## Memoir of an Immigrant Child

Cholet Kelly Josué, MD

*Twelve Unending Summers*
*Memoir of an Immigrant Child*
Cholet Kelly Josué, MD

1. BIO002000 2. BIO026000 3. BIO002010
Paperback ISBN: 978-1-949642-04-9
Ebook ISBN: 978-1-949642-05-6
Library of Congress Control Number: 2019935081

Printed in the United States of America

Authority Publishing
11230 Gold Express Dr. #310-413
Gold River, CA 95670
800-877-1097
www.AuthorityPublishing.com

# CONTENTS

# PROLOGUE

I died that day.

That is what happens when an earthquake destroys what was once your childhood paradise.

When Mother Nature paid a visit to Haiti in 2010, I died inside, as I wondered how many others would die with me that day. But what I did not expect was to also experience the cycle of life: from death would come rebirth, the flow uninterrupted and as constant as the rising and setting sun. Out of that catastrophe emerged a question of identity that had been simmering inside me for decades, after having spent all my adult life thinking like an American, after having been assimilated into the American melting pot.

Or maybe not so assimilated after all.

Years ago, when I was doing my residency in Chicago, I was making my way through the hospital cafeteria when a tall, slender, White attending physician approached. He looked me up and down, almost as though in resignation. "Where in Africa are you from?" he finally said.

*Here we go again,* I thought: *Once more I must be reminded that although I am a medical resident, although I have lived two decades in America, even though I have returned to Haiti just once in twenty years, I am still the other.*

"Oh, let's see," I said, sounding casual. As a resident, my showing disrespect could come back to haunt me—but maybe I could have a little fun. "I was from Africa about four hundred years ago."

He looked at me, incredulous. "What do you mean?"

"I was from Africa about four hundred years ago, but I have been living in America ever since."

As he stood there confused, I looked to leave before I said something I would regret. "I am from the Caribbean, born in the Bahamas to Haitian parents."

His face contorted, and I smiled and left to rejoin my resident group.

*Where do I belong?*

I think all human beings ask this question to some extent, even without knowing; we are continuously trying to integrate ourselves. But for people like me whose lives have straddled several societies, the question of finding the true self while still feeling like the other no matter where we go is elusive, ever-evolving, and for some, never-ending. Since moving to the United States as a teenager I have been caught between assimilating fully as an American and trying to negotiate and retain other parts of myself that are indispensable to me: my birthplace in the Bahamas, and Haiti, where I spent twelve years of a simple and decent if checkered childhood. I cannot belong solely to any of these three places, but all three are essential to who I have been and who I will become. As the great poet Maya Angelou, who was so comfortable in her skin, once said, "I belong everywhere and nowhere."

Juggling multiple identities and cultures brings with it the breadth of human experience: serious challenges but also great opportunities. Now I must rearrange those experiences into a new place that I can call home.

# 1

## HERE WE GO AGAIN

"Cholet, did you see? CNN just reported an earthquake in Haiti."

I could not tell if the words were coming from my head or from the other end of the phone. Then I felt the pressure of the phone against the palm of my left hand and realized it was an actual voice on the line. "Are you sure?" I said.

"Yes, Cholet, and it looks bad."

"Okay, okay, I'll take a look."

But I was not about to turn on the news right away.

I had just gotten home from a long, tiring day at work. It was one of those crisp and cold but sunny January days in Maryland, when the frigid air makes the indoors feel bigger and emptier than usual. The once-green grass on the hill outside my home was yellow and dead; the raspy trill of the American sparrow was long gone from my windowsill. The fear of what I might see was a heavy weight keeping me in place.

The sun was setting early in Baltimore this winter day, but daylight still lingered in Haiti, I knew. Inside my apartment, the air was cold and still—remarkably quiet. You could cut it with a knife and there would be no trace of the blade.

Minutes later, I received a second phone call, this time from my younger sister, Marthe.

"Did you hear there is an earthquake in Port-au-Prince? I have been trying unsuccessfully to reach Luckson; I cannot get through."

Among my many family members living in Port-au-Prince, my youngest brother, Luckson, was foremost in my mind. I was also thinking of my first, best childhood friend, my cousin Will, still in Haiti. I had seen them both just six weeks earlier during my last trip there. I hoped they were all okay. The prospect of something else was too much for me to contemplate.

I talked briefly to Marthe, asking how she was, but I did not want to inquire more. The only thing I wanted was a nap, and to wake up later, refreshed and relieved to discover that the earthquake was all a misunderstanding. I struggled to relax on the couch, reaching out for the remote control that was even colder in my hand than the phone. I hesitated several times before turning on the TV.

Haiti had been in the news continuously for the past thirty years or so for one catastrophe or another or because of some political turmoil. For a while, it seemed as if we had a coup d'état every week. I was tired of the bad news, and the international community, rightfully, was becoming tired of helping; they had sent Haiti hundreds of millions of dollars since the fall of Baby Doc in 1986. To this day, no one can tell where all that money went.

I was proud of my roots, but none of us wants only bad news coming out of our homeland. When I left South Florida to go to medical school in Atlanta, one silver lining in that cultural shift was that because of the distance, I could pick and choose when I wanted to check on the news in the Haitian community there. And during that time, there was a lot of bad news, not the least of which were dead Haitians washing up on the South Florida shoreline. Sometimes I could even make believe that the trials and tribulations the Haitian diaspora was experiencing within the United States and on the mainland of Haiti were not real.

The moment the TV clicked on, I heard the crackling of huge white columns crumbling into a thick cloud of white dust. I was watching the destruction of the Haitian palace, the most iconic building in Haiti and one of the most beautiful palaces in the Caribbean, if not in all of the Americas. Out of all the buildings in Haiti the palace stood above the rest, and I always thought it to be indestructible. Who could have expected this huge palace to crumble so fast?

Before I could process what I was seeing, another scene flashed onto the screen, and for a few moments I felt like I was there, inside the action. I leaned forward as though to touch them, to be among the crowd. A throng of people, mostly women, appeared, all dressed in white robes, the devastation, grief, and shock showing on their faces as they walked down the main road in front of the US embassy with both hands held up and arms wide open. They were singing in unison, as if calling on God—and the Americans—to have pity on them.

I sat back. *Here we go again*, I thought: *We Haitians are begging the White men with their "White God" to come and save us from yet another catastrophe.*

The procession stopped and the singing grew louder. I turned up the volume as I watched the people's faces becoming more grief stricken—almost as if they were acting, putting on a show, and that is exactly what was happening. I think as soon as they saw the TV cameras they started singing, shouting, and kneeling down because they knew how to send a message to the outside world.

I sat frozen in the middle of my living room, caught in an out-of-body experience that whisked me across the continent and out to sea. For one moment, I was in the middle of that crowd with them, feeling their helplessness and hopelessness, caught up in that same conviction that we would never be able to help ourselves.

*Here we go again.*

When you come from a place whose birth was the result of the tragedy of slavery, you don't want outsiders to see you naked and vulnerable. Seeing people who looked like me—like my aunts, cousins, and nieces—filing in front of the American embassy, singing to the CNN cameras with open arms, asking for help, made the wounds of our tragedies one inch deeper.

I hated the fact that they were playing the same refrain that we Haitians had been using for centuries, because we have been conditioned to see ourselves as helpless victims. At the same time, here I was, sitting in a cozy place, watching their misery, not mine; but being a flawed human being, my response was also about me and my pride. I was embarrassed for them and for myself, and yet I was not in their shoes, feeling their devastating loss. I was safe inside my apartment in Maryland.

I knew my anger was misdirected at these poor, mostly uneducated people, whose only crime was that they lived in a country whose corrupt leaders have all but abandoned their people for the past two hundred years. What choice did they have but to ask outsiders for help, when all their lives their government has never adequately provided for them? These people were braver, more hopeful, and more resilient than their leaders, who were mostly foreign-educated in some of the best universities in the world.

I, too, was foreign in a way. I had left Haiti for Miami on a wooden boat twenty-five years before, and it was only during my most recent trip to Haiti, six weeks before the earthquake—only my second trip back—that I felt ready to acknowledge myself as belonging there once again. I hadn't realized when I left my friends, my village, to come to America, and even for years afterward, that during my childhood Haiti was the right place for me. Here among my own people, with my own tribe, I had received the confidence and self-esteem, the sense of collective community and belonging vital for any child to grow into a stable, functioning adult.

And yet South Florida became the perfect place for my teenage years and young adulthood. America represented that free space and fertile ground where I could develop my faculty for critical thinking and attempt to reach my potential. Both the United States and Haiti were intimately connected to the person I had become, both existentially indispensable in my life. If Haiti and America did not exist, I would have had to invent them.

The past few years had brought with them a slowly emerging understanding that all three countries—the Bahamas, Haiti, the United States—were fully part of who I was and who I would become. I had begun to entertain in my mind's eye the notion that maybe, just maybe, amid America and the Bahamas and Haiti, I might create a home where I could totally, truly belong.

Then the earthquake came and shattered that dream.

I stepped away from the TV for a moment, trying to distract myself. I did not want to know, and yet I did. I had to. I bolted back into the living room when I heard the CNN anchor reporting the latest images from Haiti. Transfixed, I saw an image on the screen that still haunts me: a lone soul, a tall man running about the palace amid the dust and smoke, with walls and ceiling pieces crumbling all around him. He went first in one direction, then abruptly turned back when he saw the ceiling fully collapse. I still wonder what happened to this man. Did he make it out alive? Did he have a wife and children? What became of him? Did his family ever know?

# 2

# A PLACE TO BELONG

By the time I began my medical training in Chicago, it had been more than twenty years since I stepped onto the shores of Miami, my home throughout my teenage years and into young adulthood. I had certainly experienced challenges in South Florida—living undocumented, barely on the edge of society, trying to make ends meet—but South Florida's tropical climate and the large Caribbean population, more specifically the large Haitian immigrant population, had never left a question in my mind that the United States was where I belonged. In fact, I considered myself a fully assimilated American, and why not? I spent my teenage years here. I ate apple pie, Bojangles chicken, and KFC, and I enjoyed the county fairs and the movies, just like any other American kid.

Chicago was different. The hot tropical sun that gives me energy was gone. There were no palm trees to remind me of Haiti, even when I tried to forget it, and the warm, soothing breezes of the Atlantic Ocean were replaced by a persistent chilly wind blowing in from Lake Michigan. I sat inside the university library one afternoon, resting comfortably where the benches met the window, and waited for my freezing brain to warm up. I had just walked in after braving the bone-chilling cold of Chicago in mid-February, when even crossing the parking lot makes you do things you normally don't do unless you feel like your life is in danger, like reciting the Lord's Prayer five or six times to convince your body with each step that it's not as bitter cold as it seems. But now, as I delved into my exam review materials, a soothing warmth touched my back. I turned to see the faint yellow glow of the sun amid a sea of gray clouds—a welcome sight during winter in Chicago, when the sky often was morose, depressed, overcast.

*Hi, friend, where have you been, Mr. Sun? We have not seen each other for the past ten days.*

Fond memories of the Haitian sun flowed into my mind then from another place and time, when I played soccer, when I ran up and down the rolling fields of sunflowers in rural Haiti—memories I would rather not have dwelled on while I was busy studying for a difficult medical exam. I felt the pressure of my body against the cold surface of the chair and forced my eyes to the white papers in front of me, but the warm glow of the Caribbean sunshine came flooding back into my mind. And even as I wished I could escape these thoughts of bygone years, the visions of rolling sunflower meadows and days spent chasing mourning doves with my cousin Will overwhelmed me. I put the papers aside.

*  *  *

I had moved from Atlanta to the Midwest in 2003 to start my medical residency at the University of Illinois at Chicago. The Windy City was several thousand miles from the Caribbean, but it felt light-years away, and it seemed almost a century had passed since the last day I'd spent in Haiti as a teenager. I recalled picnicking by the beach in my coastal hometown, playing volleyball with my soccer team, and eating mangoes and corn on the cob in the soothing, salty breeze of the Caribbean. Life was good for us young people then, and it was only going to get better. Or so we thought.

Almost ten years had passed since my last trip to Haiti, my first trip back, which came right before I moved to Atlanta to start medical school.

Even then I knew the country had changed; when I lived in South Florida, the daily news was full of Haiti's political turmoil and the unending drama of rickety boats washing up on the Florida shores. But as I approached from the air on that first trip back, I cringed. The houses appeared to tilt precariously below me, leaning against one another like dominoes in disorder. The calm inside the plane, along with the eerie silence of the passengers, belied what lay beneath—devastation, grief, and abject poverty.

As we drove away from the airport, I realized that the devastation was a hundred times worse than I had thought. Delmas, a street that used to be clean and well paved, looked like a tank had driven through it, leaving craters every few yards. The dilapidated houses had bricks falling off them left and right, and the place was full of so many people it looked like an army of ants milling about. The pungent smell of misery pervaded the stale, hot, humid air. It was hard to breathe, let alone think.

Had it always been like this, with houses built in such disorder? No, Port-au-Prince in the mid-1980s was orderly, as I remembered it; or maybe we did not have as many houses or people then, and everything fell apart after the fall of Baby Doc. In the wake of the uprising, countless families had moved from the countryside to the city, and because of corruption the zoning codes were not applied, which meant you could build your house anywhere. I knew from the news what had happened since I had come to America in 1984, but still I could not reconcile the sight of this Haiti with the Haiti I had thought was waiting for me.

After that first trip in 1998, I tried to bury the painful memories in the back of my mind. It was as if I hoped the passage of time or the busyness of medical school and residency would allow me to forget. Maybe things would look different by the time I visited again, if ever I could summon the courage to revisit all things past, all things human—loss, regret, guilt, vanishing footprints in the grass, missing people and places—the remnants of my lost childhood paradise.

So, I was surprised when right in the middle of that intensely cold Chicago winter several years later, with my tired eyes squinting at fuzzy medical material, I found myself thinking of my childhood in Haiti again.

It was not until I moved to the Midwest that I truly experienced what it was like to be living as a minority in a majority culture. I thought I had experienced culture shock when I arrived at medical school in Atlanta, one of the first times I had ventured farther north than Disney World. But living in Atlanta meant I could take a break after every eight-week test block and drive straight down to Florida. As soon as I crossed the state border the sight of palm trees brought the warm feeling that soon I would be home.

I liked Chicago, with its wide-open, clean streets and awe-inspiring architecture. Even now I tell friends it is the American city that feels most European. Yet this city, and the Midwest also, seemed to represent the real America, so unlike the multicultural community I knew from South Florida. In some ways, Chicago is quite diverse, with Mexican, Polish, Greek, and Italian immigrants, but often it seemed only two cultures existed: White American and Black American. I spent most of my day at the hospital among the majority White population, and my social life was focused on the Urban League of Young Black Professionals and Trinity United Church of Christ, with Reverend Jeremiah Wright. But in neither setting could I fully belong; in fact, time after time I was mistaken for Nigerian or some lost tribe from a nameless African country. I was told that my protruding cheekbones gave me away as being West African. The whole time I had lived in South Florida, with its large Haitian population, my Haitian roots were never mistaken.

Here even the doctors asked me where in Africa I was from.

*I am a medical resident who reached adulthood in America. Yet I am still the other.*

Living in the Midwest made it clear that I was not fully American after all, despite being an American citizen—despite living here for more than two decades. Then again, my 1998 trip to Haiti had left me feeling distanced from my childhood as well, although at that time I could not verbalize what I was feeling. A trip to the Bahamas earlier in 2007 resulted in much the same emotions. I remember walking up to the huge steps of Princess Margaret Hospital, where I had been told I was born, looking for a lifeline of memory that could connect me to the land of my birthplace. After a few minutes I left feeling sad, an errant bohemian with no real place to call my own. The questions came fast and furious: Who am I? Where do I belong? Can I ever find a place, both physically and in my mind, where I feel I fully belong?

All my life, I have been aware of the many identities I have collected. I was born in the Bahamas before it became independent, which made me a British subject with Bahamian citizenship. And though I understood why my parents originally moved our family to Haiti—the mistreatment of Haitian immigrants in the Bahamas was common and they did not want their children to be seen as less than equal—I never questioned my acceptance in the Bahamas. Perhaps I did not think about it much after we moved to Haiti. I was only four years old, after all.

As for Haiti, there is no question the best part of my life was the three years we spent there together as a family. Although I acknowledge I have romanticized my childhood experiences in Haiti somewhat, and life was much more checkered than I have wanted to believe, to me Haiti was a living paradise. Even after the death of my dad and my mother's subsequent absence, overall my community remained intact. My social environment, including my beloved elementary school, did not change; and in time I almost forgot that I was not born there. I looked forward to stepping onto the beautiful manicured green grass of my elementary school, looking up at its imposing white columns and its tall walls lined with hibiscus. On weekends, I spent time at my aunt's house with Will, running through nature and playing soccer for hours on end, as if time did not exist.

In Miami, questions of identity, race, and ethnicity began to take shape, something that seems specific to living in America. In fact, I did not know how Haitian I was until I moved to South Florida. That's when I started hearing derogatory things like "Haitians stink" and "those boat people." Sometimes, Haitian kids would lie about where they were born, saying they were not born in Haiti but in the Bahamas. That was the first time I became conscious of how much I loved Haiti, so almost without thinking I began to claim that I was born in Haiti, even though I was not. I was not going to disown the country where my DNA was made, where my parents and all those who gave me a community had allowed me to believe in myself, affording me dreams enough to fill my pockets, and then some.

But even amid Miami's diverse, multicultural, and colorful community—even with the racial tension between American kids and us newcomers—I never felt different enough to question my identity on a deeper level. After all, most of the people I hung out with were either fresh off the boat or children of parents from the Caribbean or Latin America themselves, or they came from the many countries that make up the distinct South Florida part of the big American melting pot.

I was used to living in a country where things are done in an orderly way, and in fact, looking back now, even before I set foot in the United States, I felt a kinship with the ideas that no one is above the law, order must be adhered to, and your station in life is not determined by where you were born or the family from which you came, but by your positive character traits and capacity for hard work. Those seeds were planted at an early age by the fact that I was born in the Bahamas, the family that raised me, and the formal education I received from the Christian Brothers' school. In fact, visiting Haiti right before I left for medical school showed me just how much I had changed myself and how I had come to view the world through an American lens.

And yet despite all this, the outside world saw me merely as a foreign Black man with strong African features and an accent, as if my life here for more than twenty years counted for nothing.

What did that mean? How American was I if other Americans did not recognize me as one of them?

I was not American enough, and perhaps I was not Bahamian enough either. When we left the Bahamas for Haiti, I was too young to be issued a passport, and whatever birth certificate my parents had as proof of my citizenship had been lost. Although Haitian society had never been anything but fully accepting of all kids born to Haitian parents anywhere, I questioned if not being born in Haiti made me less than truly Haitian. If I were fully Haitian, would I have left Haiti, or would I have stayed there, like my four childhood friends who never left the country even when they had ample opportunity? Perhaps subconsciously I envied my best friends who were born in Haiti and never intended to leave. Was it in their DNA that they were destined to live there? Even from a very young age I was aware I might leave Haiti one day, and that sense of being rudderless became stronger once I left Haiti for America.

I was overwhelmed that day in the Chicago library, as my mind pulled me back to places I would rather not go. But how else could I answer the questions that had haunted me? *Where did I fully belong? Where could I call home?*

I was not yet ready to accept my past and step into my own sense of belonging in all the places I have lived. I could only hope to synthesize all these experiences in my mind, mostly the positive ones, to analyze them, and to make myself feel more at home. Perhaps someday I might acknowledge that I could belong in all these places at the same time. Or maybe, just maybe, I could belong perfectly to all these places in their own ways.

# 3

# CAN WE EVER GO HOME AGAIN?

An uncomfortable silence moved through the wide-bodied Airbus as it descended under a sunny blue sky over the city of Port-au-Prince. I could only hear the changing speed of the airplane, but below us the calm turquoise bay of the capital seemed peaceful, like a comfortable, cool blue mattress, with barely any activity on the bay except for two or three huge cargo ships awaiting the tugboats to guide them in. Further in the distance I could just make out the city—with the random disorder of the houses I knew awaited me.

I was landing in Haiti a second time since I had left as a teenager, a little more than a decade after my first trip back. Then I'd been shocked by the devastation from the political instability since the fall of the Duvalier dictatorship. But today I had made my mind a blank slate, returning with no preconceived notions of what to expect. Instead, I focused on my own burgeoning awakening of self-awareness—my search to belong in a place where I did not feel like "the other."

Perhaps this is the angst all Haitians living abroad feel when we return to Haiti. Those of us who have lived in more lawful, organized societies are aware of the canyon-size contrast with Haiti—the lawlessness and corruption accompanying the unpredictability and fragility of human life. At any moment, riots may erupt and flights will be canceled so that no one can get in or out for days. This had been normal in Haiti since the mid- to late 1980s, after the fall of Baby Doc. Among the diaspora, we have a joke: if you go to Haiti and get in trouble, remember no one will be able to bail you out. In fact, some of us view going back to Haiti as a risk or even a sacrifice, as it means leaving our comfortable lives behind, if only for a short while.

In an act of defiance, I refused to see it like that. How was my life more valuable than that of the people from whom I came? How could I be more worthy than my brother, cousins, and family, whose only crime, if one may call it that, was that they lacked an American passport?

As soon as the plane stopped on the tarmac and I was firmly on Haitian ground, I put myself in that state of mind—as if I had never left. I had not expected these feelings, not after my first experience returning to Haiti all those years earlier. But this time was different. I tried to act like I belonged there. I found out over the course of the trip that everyone could tell I had been away from Haiti for a long while. They could see it in my eyes, hear it in my voice, and smell it on my skin. Yet in my head, the moment I landed in Haiti I belonged there fully, and no one was going to tell me otherwise.

I went to Haiti for a variety of reasons, both conscious and unconscious. I wanted to visit with my brother Luckson and my cousin Will to catch up on the long years since we had seen each other, but more than that, I wanted to see Haiti with new eyes. I needed to witness firsthand the land, the people, and the few things that had not changed since I had left. I was hungry to smell the air and hear the barking of wild dogs and the rooster's song early in the morning. I had to experience the things I had lost or blocked from my mind since I moved to the United States.

It felt like an eternity had passed since that trip I had made just before medical school, even since my time in Chicago for residency training. Now, I was a newly minted physician, practicing medicine in Maryland and looking for a sense of purpose greater than myself. I was traveling with a group of friends who had undertaken a grand project: to build a school system from elementary to university, and eventually a Level I trauma hospital complex. During this trip, we would witness the inauguration of the elementary school in Leogane, a coastal town about thirty minutes by car from the capital and almost seven hours by car from Saint-Louis-du-Nord, the small coastal town where I grew up. We also operated a small medical clinic doing basic checkups for the parents of the schoolchildren. It was the happiest I had been and felt about myself, and I was hopeful for the future.

Hope had been a hard commodity to come by for the past thirty years.

The night before the inauguration, something took me by surprise when I visited a friend. I smelled food that I had not experienced for so long, something we call *tassot*. Made from goat meat, *tassot* is a national dish where the meat is fried and picked apart by hand, fiber by fiber, like spaghetti. When I arrived at my friend's house, I introduced myself to the whole family and then used my nose to find where the food was being cooked. I was behaving just as I had done as a child, when my friends and I would move around the house strategically like hound dogs, hunting by smell, drawn by the sweet aroma of ripening mangoes in the attic.

Once I found the goat meat, I took a little chair and sat as close to the pot as possible, hoping for as many nuggets as possible to come my way. And as I smelled and tasted the familiar flavors, as always happens when I visit Haiti, bittersweet childhood memories came flooding into my brain: happy because I loved these things as a child, but also sad because once I left Haiti, I stopped craving or even wanting Haitian food. But I was not about to ruin the night, so just as quickly I suppressed those memories, as I often did when reminded of the childhood I had left behind.

The next morning, my colleagues and I got up early for the inauguration. The sun was becoming warmer and the fading morning breeze carried the voices of merchants yelling for people to buy their products in the street. This is how Haitian mornings start, with a cacophony of seemingly disorganized yet synchronized movements of people who have acted that way for a hundred years. I thought of the hometown that I had not been to since I left. I was sure that the people, the landscape, and the houses would all be unrecognizable. This is one of the tragedies of mass migration, of being uprooted; you lose everything, even your sense of place. Yet I was still here in Haiti among people I loved, and I was part of something good, bigger than myself, beyond the scope of politics and misplaced pride.

We rode together to the inauguration in an SUV, and as the vehicle strained to make its way up the steep mountain where the school was built, I saw huge tents with blue tops and white sides emerging in the distance. The crowd had already gathered and the weather was hot, but a faint breeze made it tolerable if you could find a hint of shade. The school was a beautiful yellow two-story building, perched at the highest point of elevation in the city of Leogane, on a mountain dominating the landscape. From this vantage point, you could survey vast fields of sugarcane and bananas as far as the eye could see.

It seemed like the who's who of Haiti were present that day—including all the major newspapers and a couple of TV stations. I was overwhelmed to be among people doing tangible good, feeling lucky to be part of it. I almost questioned if it was real.

The night before, a few of us had ventured out into the city in a brand-new Toyota Land Cruiser Prado. As we cruised up and down the streets, I heard the driver saying in a hush-hush voice that the SUV belonged to the fleet of the interior minister, who was a friend of the family or something like that. I have to admit that although I decried the relentless corruption that was sinking Haitian society, I couldn't help feeling pleased that I had friends with people in the corridors of power. As a Black kid growing up in the US—as a Black immigrant with an accent, in fact—I had subconsciously accepted my fate, meaning that I had understood I had a certain place in society, perceived or real. So that night, it felt good to be treated better than the norm rather than worse.

Despite my feelings, I knew that back in America you did not have to be close to people in power to access the necessities of daily life. In both Haiti and the US, education could be the key to a better life. This was something I had experienced for myself and I hoped this new school and center would open up new opportunities for the children attending it, just as I had been given a head start by attending the Christian Brothers' elementary school. Seeing the beautiful, happy faces of these kids, I was overcome with hope that they would have a chance to reach their potential. One of the greatest gifts you can give a child anywhere, but especially in a country like Haiti, is a solid education in the formative years.

For a few moments, as I gazed out at the abundant valley, I thought about the school in my hometown, my friends, the places we used to go, and the things we talked about as children. Then I snapped back into the moment of the inauguration. *What's the point remembering my hometown? After all, I am not going there this time.* In fact, I had not been there since the day I left for the US. I stayed for the entire ceremony, mingling with the other guests until after sunset. Then I made the long drive back to my hotel, feeling a mix of pride, excitement, melancholy, and exhaustion.

The day after the inauguration, Luckson, my cousin Augustin, and I got up early and drove to the American embassy, where Luckson hoped to get a visa to come study in the US the following year. As we approached, the unending line of people snaking around the front walls of the embassy told me we were in for a long day, but I was not prepared for how painful it would become, emotionally and physically. I let Luckson out of the car so he could get a good place in line, and it did not take him long to make it inside the embassy courtyard. This was just one of several steps to reach the actual location where they held the visa interviews.

While Augustin and I waited in the car, we watched with growing anger how the guards treated the people—my people—*us.* The Haitian nationals, hired by the American embassy for security, were yelling at their fellow Haitians standing in the hot sun. I thought of my teenage years in South Florida, and how Black Haitian immigrants were treated with less consideration than others. I'd come to Haiti in part to feel good about being an American citizen and a Haitian, and now I was enraged. At that moment I had disdain for all things American—the guards, the embassy, the staff in the air-conditioned spaces inside.

And yet I was American myself. I sat in my car feeling small and insignificant.

When my brother reemerged around five o'clock from behind the big beige embassy wall, I knew from his walk that he was not getting the visa. The inauguration, the smells and sights and sounds of Haiti, and the ride in the fancy car—all that joy vanished, transformed into helplessness and sadness. Here I was, an American doctor with an American passport, but all of that did not mean a thing in Haiti if I was not connected at the highest level.

*   *   *

That trip to Haiti left me even more confused than when I had visited as a young man about to enter medical school. True, it was no longer the same Haiti, but I had known that going in. And it was never really about the land. It was about the people, the heart of the country, and the smells and sounds, and the well-worn paths I used to trample so long ago that only fragments and fuzzy pictures remained in my mind. Visiting Haiti was about me and my own need to belong there fully again—to belong somewhere, to be distinct yet not feel like I am "the other."

I was both sad and relieved to leave Haiti and return to my comfortable life, the guilt almost suffocating as I stood in the long line of passengers waiting to board the American Airlines flight back to Miami. I had sacrificed comfort to spend a few days in the land of my childhood, with the dusty traffic, the stench of abject poverty under the hot burning sun, the sunken faces of women and children in the heat, and I had come up empty-handed. I kept saying to myself, "I don't understand why they're smiling. I don't know why these people choose to be alive."

At the same time, my medical work during the trip had opened up a new way of thinking for me, something I had never experienced. I had not realized how different it was to restore the health of someone who looks like you and speaks in your own mother's language, or how it would give me a unique sense of purpose I had not felt while practicing medicine in the United States. In the US, my connections to patients operated more at arm's length, but here—here it was personal.

The experience with my brother at the embassy had shown me a different side of who I was and my place in Haitian society. It was the beginning of an awareness that after so many years living in the States, I was no longer the same person. Now I had multiple identities and could never belong to one at a time; I was going to have to integrate these three identities into a new comfortable self. I needed a new place to call home, a stable platform combining my life and experience into some place where I could fully belong, even if it only existed in my mind.

As the Airbus picked up speed, the runway disappearing and the airport terminal becoming smaller and smaller in the distance, I made a promise to myself. While America would always be a part of me, I would find a connection to Haiti too. Perhaps I would do health care there, which had already filled me with an organic, genuine sense of purpose. Maybe I could have the best of both worlds, which were only located a short plane ride apart.

* * *

Just six weeks later Haiti suffered one of the worst disasters in its history, the January 12, 2010, earthquake that left a swath of destruction throughout the nation. The epicenter was in Leogane, and our beautiful school and its symbol of hope was completely destroyed. Luckily, there were no children at the school at that time.

When I heard later that this beautiful yellow school, which reminded me so much of my own elementary school, was gone with little chance of rebuilding, my heart hurt. I could see the children frolicking during the inauguration and a shadow of myself taking it all in. I relived the joy around me, the assured realization that I was part of something bigger than myself, the hope that I could contribute to the well-being of women and children by working toward a decent health care system and education. Could it really be true that all of that had been dashed?

With the buildings fell my dreams and hopes of creating change in Haiti. As the happy faces of those little children appeared before my eyes, I thought about what would become of their future. They had started out so hopeful. But hope is often crushed in a moment of tragedy. And the school was not the only thing that would need to be rebuilt.

# 4

# "STUPID ROTTEN HAITIANS!"

In Haiti, when someone dies and their situation was a sad one, people will say that person "died of melancholia," regardless of whether the person had been suffering from a chronic terminal illness. When I woke up in the hospital one time as a little boy and realized I was not going to go home right away with my mother, I felt that same melancholic pain, as if I were going to die myself. Of course, a child's perception of pain and death is limited by the young brain's living experiences—a lot of things can look and feel catastrophic, and we human beings do not do well anytime our place of comfort is disturbed. My mother was my world at that moment, and when she left my hospital room, I didn't understand how the world could keep on going without her by my side.

Family legend has it that when I was about three and a half years old, I threw myself under a moving car. I lost consciousness and had to be rushed to the hospital. Please don't judge me; aren't we all crazy and reckless at three years old?

I heard this story over and over as a child, whenever I would try to be mischievous, as I often was growing up in my little part of coastal Haiti, in the northwestern part overlooking the huge Atlantic Ocean. My family would warn me to be careful, telling me how much trouble I had already caused.

"This is why your parents ran off with you to Haiti," an aunt or a cousin would say. "They left the Bahamas so you wouldn't kill yourself."

I would laugh at the story then; I felt powerful to have caused an entire family to move to another country. All kids at that age want to believe that they control their world, that they have superpowers, but what made me more curious about the whole story was that there was proof of it: I used to live in the Bahamas, and I was now living in Haiti.

My fascination with storytelling started with this tale. Yet I don't have any recollection of the accident itself. In fact, I must have had the wind knocked out of me pretty good because I did not wake up until ten or twelve hours after the incident.

At three in the morning I woke up inside a big hospital crib, tall enough that I could not crawl up to get out. I was being held in a beige room with a high ceiling that looked like it might touch the sunny Caribbean sky. The room was filled with yellow cribs, and any sense of peace there might have been was disturbed by the high-pitched shrieking of other children and the movement of nurses throughout the room. I'd woken in a strange, scary, and wondrous world, irresistibly inviting and terribly disturbing. I was not home, and my mother, whom I was always glued to, clutching her robe or whatever I could hold on to with my left hand to keep her within reach, was not there. I cried and cried, probably cried myself back to sleep, hoping all would be right with the world when I woke up.

My mom came the next morning, close to midday, and immediately I assumed things would go back to normal. She had brought clothes and food because apparently I'd been too upset to eat whatever food they had at the hospital, and I was certain that once I finished eating, I was going to go home. I mean, why not? My mother took me wherever she went, so why should this day be any different?

Instead, I was kept at the hospital for forty-eight hours for observation. From what I was told later, the doctors concluded that I was very lucky to just have the wind knocked out of me. For me, though, going home was the lucky part. I thought everything was back to normal.

Several years later, as a child growing up in Haiti, I heard the full account of what happened that morning in Nassau, in the Bahamas.

My cousin Micheline had been taking me and my sister to school. We were standing by the road, waiting for the green light to cross Wulff Road, one of Nassau's major and busiest streets, and Micheline was holding our hands. It was rush hour and Nassau was one of the busiest economic centers in the

Caribbean, the financial capital and the seat of the Bahamian government. The tourism sector was developing quickly, and direct foreign investment had already experienced significant growth in the 1960s and 1970s, along with the harvesting of the Bahamian pine forests to make pulp and paper and furniture for England. Immigrants from Jamaica and Haiti had established themselves in Nassau, and the growing Bahamian middle class were becoming consumers of goods, like cars, and multiple services.

We had been waiting a few minutes at the intersection, surrounded by the revving of engines, the smell of gasoline, and the heat of the exhaust in the air, all under the glistening rays of the rising Caribbean sun. You could feel the tension, I imagine, but none of us knew what the morning would bring or cared.

"I bet you I can throw myself under this car," I said, according to my cousin.

I am not sure why I said that or why I even thought of doing such a ridiculous thing. I had tons of energy at home, keen to be everywhere and get into everything, so my mom spent a lot of time trying to keep me on a short leash. I moved quickly when I got an idea in my head—so by the time my cousin was reaching for my hand, I was already lying unconscious under the car that was just about to pick up speed. The driver probably got the daylights scared out of her when she discovered she'd almost killed a little kid. Here she was, minding her business on her way to work, when I showed up and turned her morning upside down. According to Micheline, the woman jumped out of the car, looked down at me, and screamed.

"Fucking Haitian!"

At that time, my parents had been living in Nassau for about six years among a growing and restless Haitian diaspora in the Bahamas. Our house was always bustling, with my mother cooking for my father's fellow workmen, most of whom had left their families back in Haiti. The men would gather in the front yard, playing dominoes and cards and talking, doing the things they normally would do back home to build community, even as they planned to return to Haiti someday.

By the time my parents' generation came along, Haiti's economy was a shell of what it had been. Just twenty years earlier, Haiti had finally finished paying back the money France claimed it would have made had the Haitian slaves not fought to free themselves from the hell that was slavery back in the 1800s. This "agreement" had meant that whatever plans the former slaves might have had to develop the country—public school systems, a sustainable economy, and investment in human capital—were impossible. Then for decades the leaders were mired in political infighting, so they failed to create an infrastructure where the people could thrive and ply their trades.

Haiti also had a growing population that it could not feed. The explosion of young, largely uneducated people like my parents, full of energy and potential but for whom the country held no viable future, is normally a recipe for political instability. It also causes a dislocation of the population. People like my parents, who had neither the education nor the ambition to create political strife, began looking to nearby islands for a better future. They left in droves, which I am sure took the pressure off, easing tensions for the Haitian politicians.

At the same time, British colonies like the Bahamas were developing quickly. Britain needed raw materials for its economy, and the Bahamian pine forest was a valuable resource. Industrious young men like my dad could make a good living working the forest cutting trees, logging from sunup to sundown. Women with trades like my mother, who was a seamstress, served the growing migrant Haitian population. Later, my mother also cooked for the men working with my dad who had not brought their wives to the Bahamas or were single and did not have time to do anything but work all day.

My parents met in the Bahamas a few years before I was born. By the time of my accident, they had four children, and our life there was pretty good. My dad had managed to buy two used cars, and we had even moved to one of the prime streets in the area, Wulff Road—something my mom mentioned all the time when we were back in Haiti.

But raising children without one's own village or tribe can make family life more difficult. Immigrants who have left their community back in their native land have to make a new community, which may be harder to do than they expected. Even when my mom sent for one of her nieces from Haiti to come and help her, she, like many of her friends in the Haitian diaspora, faced a new reality that she and my father may not have conceived of beforehand.

The Haitian migrant population was increasing fast in the Bahamas, which created friction between them and the native Bahamians on the already small island of Nassau, where more than seventy percent of the Bahamian population lived. The vast majority of Haitian migrants came from a poor country looking for better opportunities, but the Bahamian natives were also looking for opportunities to better their lives and those of their children. That meant they might have seen Haitian migrants as unwanted invaders, competing for resources they needed. The fact that the Haitians spoke a different language and shared a different culture—a contrast to the migrants from English-speaking places like Jamaica—made it harder for them to be accepted by Bahamian natives.

After all, the fear of the unknown naturally raises anxiety in the human brain.

But it went beyond a clash of cultures. The 1960s were changing times throughout the British Empire, and like the people of many African countries, Bahamians were also beating the drum of self-determination. In particular they wanted to change the laws that they had been living under for hundreds of years, and that included immigration laws. They had no say in the immigration policies of their country, including the increase of migrant workers like the Haitians.

With the tension growing between the Haitian immigrants and the native Bahamians, my parents and some of their friends were becoming uneasy raising their children in what seemed to be an increasingly hostile place. Many were already thinking of going back home to Haiti, while others talked of moving to America instead.

Men like my dad did not leave their country to come and have fun while living indefinitely in a foreign land. For the most part, their goal was to come and earn a living and build a sustainable life for themselves and their families with the hope of someday returning to their native land. My dad would go back to his hometown in Haiti at least twice a year to tend to his family business, buying lands and maintaining his family's estate.

In fact, by the time of my accident in Nassau, my parents had already bought a house in Saint-Louis-du-Nord back in Haiti, and my dad had substantially increased his land holdings in his hometown. They were preparing, knowing once the Bahamians gained independence, things were going to be different. My parents knew they were going back home within a year or two, but they probably had not settled on a specific date.

When the Bahamian driver called me a "fucking Haitian," that did it for my parents. They made the decision to go back to Haiti six months later. And that would become the place where I spent a checkered but happy childhood for the next twelve years, until my uncle shipped me to America.

# 5

# MY TREE OF LIFE

By my third year living in Haiti, I had settled in so well that I barely remembered I had recently barged into the country with my parents. That summer, memories of the Bahamas were distant. We were all together, my whole family, in our summer home in La Rivière des Nègres, some thirty minutes by foot from the city of Saint-Louis-du-Nord. We had two houses in Haiti. For most of the year, my mother stayed with us kids in Saint-Louis-du-Nord so we could attend school, but my dad was the sole breadwinner and his income was mainly from agriculture and farming the land, so he lived in our house in the countryside to tend to his farmlands. He would come to the city on weekends throughout the school year and return to the countryside Sunday afternoon. I called his house our summer home because we kids mainly spent time there when school was closed for the summer or we had more than two or three days of school holidays. But it was my father's birthplace and my ancestral home, the place where I was known by my family name.

Sometimes when I visited La Rivière des Nègres, I would take a trip into town to help with the shopping. The person with whom I was traveling would only have to mention my father's name and immediately everyone knew who I was. I liked the feeling then, that I was part of something greater than myself, that I did not just drop from the sky, and I feel it still—the sense that I belonged to that place, even before I knew it physically.

I still remember when my dad explained it to me, the year I turned seven. One warm morning in La Rivière des Nègres, my dad took me to the northwest side of the house and showed me four coconut trees. Given their size, I thought they must have been planted about six to eight months earlier.

"One of these trees," he said, "is your coconut tree."

More specifically, he was referring to the coconut tree under which my umbilical cord is planted.

Shortly after we arrived in Haiti, I was rummaging through a suitcase and found four little plastic bags tightly packed together. I was about to open them when my mother rushed to stop me.

"These are umbilical cords from you and your siblings," she said.

Standing in front of the coconut tree with my father, I finally put it together. Haitians who leave their countries of origin keep an African tradition: if they have children outside Haiti, they preserve a portion of the umbilical cord until they can return to the father's native place. Then they bury the umbilical cord under a fruit-bearing tree, to link their children in a more tangible way to the country of their parents' origin. It's a way of making you a bona fide member of the tribe.

That ritual has become more significant to me in the past several years, even though I have not been to my home of spiritual origin since my dad passed away. The tree represents my fascination and longing for what I felt in that space—to belong to a physical place, a people, under the stars and among the trees, amid the sweet, fruity smell of the morning dew. Despite not having visited in nearly thirty years, the fact that my umbilical cord is part of the soil of that place makes me feel part of it too.

My parents did not leave me money or lands as my inheritance, but the act of saving my umbilical cord and planting it under a tree on their land was one of the greatest gifts they could have left me, something that decades later I could somehow latch onto as a lifeline, something that has helped me keep faith with the values of the past that have done me well in my adult life.

*   *   *

Those first three years in Haiti, and especially the summers at my ancestral home, were momentous in the way they have carried me during my whole life. Life in the countryside was exciting for a little child who gravitated toward newness, and those summers gave me something new each day to look forward to: meeting an aunt, an uncle, or distant cousins who knew my grandparents, following my cousins to nearby farms looking for ripe mangoes, and playing in the big, wide-open space of people, trees, and animals, which were new to me too. I had spent my earliest years in Nassau and most of the year now in the small city of Saint-Louis-du-Nord, which, although the streets were unpaved, was considered to be a full-blown city. My half brother, Erickson, who was about fifteen years old at that time, helped me make a little garden and plant peas, and every morning I would rush to the garden to see the pea plants burgeoning out of the ground. Some days I would spend a good hour observing the shape of morning dew droplets, putting my face in front of each one to see if I could see my own image reflecting back at me.

The countryside was also where I met siblings I had never known I had.

For children it is normal to be curious how fate got two people together to breathe you into existence. My mother did not know anything about my father before they met in the Bahamas. She implored my dad to tell her if he had a wife or any children in Haiti. My dad swore that he did not have a wife or children, but my mother eventually found out he had lied. My dad already had three children when they met, although he claimed that he no longer had any relations with their mother.

At the time, I mostly thought about the fun I could have with these other kids who were somehow part of my family too, but now I admire my mother's way of handling my father's deception. Each summer she invited my half siblings to spend the summer with us, and sometimes their mother would come for a few days too. They lived on the island of Tortuga.

We had a good life during the three summers we spent there, hanging out in the garden, exploring the town and plant life, and during the afternoons we would swim in the rivers next to my uncle's house and come home at night to a feast of storytelling. My father's house was a serious place, mystical too, and in fact, the area is legendary in Haitian history for its role during the war of independence. Even today La Rivière des Nègres is one of the most sacred voodoo sites in Haiti. Some historians say that it is one of the most sacred voodoo sites worldwide. I didn't realize any of this as a child, but I suspect now that the historical importance of that area has conditioned its residents to take life seriously. They were serious about their land. They did not laugh. Perhaps they found joy in their work.

As a child, I assumed I would follow in the footsteps of my farmer dad, but during the summer of the coconut trees, I realized he had other plans for me. He was rarely home during the day, always somewhere tending to his farms, so I tried to follow him whenever I could. One afternoon that summer, he came home early and dressed to go out, and I told him I wanted to go where he was going. My dad was a man of few words with children.

"No, you are not coming," was all he said.

I figured he did not owe me an explanation, but I wanted to know anyway, so I followed him. He did not say a word, although I am certain he heard me. The place was not far from our house, a few blocks, and as we approached, I saw a building with a round thatch roof and men gathering around. I realized it was a cock-fighting place.

My dad turned around with that look he would give you only once.

"I told you that you would not go with me, and you need to go back home right now."

Now I understand he did not want me to live his life, to be a farmer like him. He already had a plan for me to become a "brain merchant" using the pen, as Jack London said. Yet I trusted that he knew best, and I had fun at my elementary school in Saint-Louis-du-Nord, L'ecole Lammenais, the Christian Brothers' school, playing soccer with friends as any lucky kid should be. For me, school and soccer were a source of joy, stability, and comfort throughout my childhood and even today.

In fact, although I enjoyed my summers in the countryside, I always looked forward to coming back to the city of Saint-Louis-du-Nord. Sometimes I daydreamed about what my friends were doing while I was away. Though the city is only about two kilometers long, it was the perfect size for small children, and we made it ours from the start.

A few months after we moved from the Bahamas, my cousins Zack and George and I decided to occupy the city imaginatively and take it as our own. First, we would divide the houses: Zack, the oldest among us, would claim the northern part of the city up to Marche Mercredi, or Wednesday Market, an open-air market where we played soccer when it was not occupied by vendors or mechanics fixing their cars. I would claim all the houses in the middle of the city, up to the Gothic cathedral looming over Saint-Louis-du-Nord. George would have the rest of the houses, all the way down to the Saint Louis Cemetery, where the city ended.

We also divided the vibrantly decorated, privately owned commercial buses of the city that traveled to and from the capital of Port-au-Prince, carrying passengers and merchandise. We were mainly preoccupied with the artwork, which was magnificent. One of my favorites portrayed an intricately detailed mermaid smiling in the middle of the turquoise Caribbean Sea, something that has remained indelibly in my mind. It was so surrealistic and fantastical, more like the magical folktales I heard at night than anything in my own experience.

The buses were given meaningful names, either biblical or from a Haitian proverb. My uncle Franck owned a bus called Secours d'en Haut (Help from God Above), though others had superstitious names because the owner had made a contract with the devil to get the money to buy the bus. Some buses were of even more dubious origin. Usually the buses would depart the city for the capital around three or four o'clock in the morning, and when we were traveling to Port-au-Prince, we would wait on our front porch for the distinct horn of the particular bus we were to take. But sometimes an adult would whisk us inside and hurriedly close the front door of the house, hyperventilating, insisting that the passing bus was not a good one—meaning that it was associated with sorcery, or the secret societies of sorcery that were said to exist.

In Haiti, life is infused with this kind of superstition. Legend has it that one of the richest landowners of the city, let's call him Levitus, had made a contract with the devil, who made him very rich. One of the terms of the agreement was that this man must wear a long blue khaki robe in permanence, as a vow. He was middle-aged, short, and muscular with a round face, and he was fascinating to the children of the town because in our conservative society, it was not acceptable for men to wear robes like this. Not much was known about the true reason for his selective attire, but he would often have a group of kids walking behind him, and sometimes a daring child would try to lift up his robe. We were always curious if he wore anything underneath; legend had it that he did not. I was not daring enough, because I knew of the consequences from my parents. Besides, Levitus was always ready with his long brown cane to strike you and delete you from the face of the earth if you came too near.

Another person who did not seem to like children was Simone, a tall grumpy woman who lived near us. Most of the time, she stayed alone inside her house, though she would come out and chase us kids when our soccer ball bounced across her gallery. All the kids thought that Simone's house was haunted and that she was part of a secret sorcery society, but one day a long escort of Range Rovers showed up at her house. We later learned the nephew of the minister to the presidency had come to visit her. Either way, the adults warned us not to cross her path.

Usually, as long as we did not hurt or bother anyone, we were free and felt safe to roam anywhere in my hometown. This was one of the joys of my childhood. In fact, if the city and its people belonged to us children, the children of the city belonged to all the adults just as much. If you went downtown and committed an infraction, you would be punished by that neighbor and you could be sure that your parents would know what happened before you got back home. We all had a set of houses where we belonged, three or four family friends' homes where you did not need permission to enter. In fact, I still have that in South Florida—three houses of family matriarchs where you do not need to call to be invited. You just show up and you are always welcome.

That city was a gift, and as time goes by and I meet friends and family friends who used to live in Saint-Louis-du-Nord, I realize the greater significance that quaint coastal place had for so many of us, where everyone knew who you belonged to and where you came from.

# 6

# SUPERSTITION IN MY GENES

A setting sun in a clear blue sky and a cool breeze with the distinct, earthy scent of dried cow manure invading the air made the perfect atmosphere for our daily afternoon soccer match. Lucas and Amos, ages fourteen and sixteen, had come back from their daily errands, but as I was just eight years old and had stayed home with their mother the whole day, I had everything ready for our game. I'd chosen the usual four green, unripe oranges that we would use for soccer balls.

Among all sports, soccer is known as the "poor man's game." Though we were not poor by Haiti's standard, it would take five dollars and two hours for us to walk to the city and buy a soccer ball made of rubber—a ball that, though it might be more suitable for playing, got punctured far too easily. Then we would need another five dollars and another long trip to the city to buy a second ball. The more practical and better option was to invent our own soccer balls from nature, as far as our ingenuity could take us.

I always looked forward to playing with these two boys. That summer, I was lucky enough to spend a few months in the countryside with one of my mother's closest friends, Ms. Nali, and her sons became my big brothers. Lucas and Amos had grown up in the countryside, so I often felt inept compared to them as we toured the woods and streams near their home. They were masters of their environment and knew the animals and the land so well that they often left me behind on their errands and adventures. They didn't want my inexperience to slow them down. But I was a very skilled soccer player.

The boys had grown up without the same open space or flat fields for soccer pitches that we enjoyed in the city. In their part of the countryside, most wide-open space was used for farmland—we played our games in the dirt front yard of their house. That made it hard for them to do much conditioning. Playing in the city, by comparison, I had developed the speed and endurance to run fast and hard, and I liked having the chance to outplay older kids and beat them every afternoon.

Each day, the game started once they showed up, Lucas and I against Amos, who was older than both of us. One day, I received a pass on the left side, and like a crouching tiger I was ready: even before Lucas gave me the ball, I had made up my mind that I would kick it with everything I had and score our first goal. The greenish-yellow orange rolled gently toward me, and I wound up for the kick of a lifetime. With my eyes on the goalposts, I decidedly was not watching for rocks or gravel that might lie buried beneath the yellow dirt.

I have always been known to have a pretty good left kick, and when the orange came at me that day, I must have unearthed everything below it, too. I immediately felt a stinging sensation, followed by warmth, traveling up my foot. That's when I knew something really bad had happened. I tried not to look—if I did not look, I would not see how bad it was, and that way I wouldn't get upset or cry—but I could not resist. When I saw my whole toenail lifted away from the nailbed and the blood spurting out like the head of a snake spitting fire, I shrieked so loudly that Ms. Nali left the food she was cooking and came running over. She scooped me up and whisked me inside. Since my mother left me in her care, she was determined that nothing should happen to me. She would do everything she could to keep me from losing even one hair—or one toenail—while I was at her house. I knew she would take care of me.

First, she washed the wound, then she poured on this god-awful alcohol that felt like I was about to get my big toe cut off. She grated unripe plantain to apply to the wound and wrapped it with clean white cotton. Once the pasty white plantain was applied, the sharp edge of the pain dissipated, replaced by an emerging sadness: I realized I would not be playing soccer for the rest of my stay with them. I did all I could to keep from crying more.

My soccer adventure was over. By the time my big toe healed, it would be time for me to go home to the city and return to school.

Although that afternoon ended in disaster, I wasn't fazed for long. I was thinking about the next exciting adventure, which, as it was approaching evening, was our nightly storytelling.

After we finished dinner and made sure the animals were properly tied up for the night, we would gather in the warmth of the kerosene lamp in the living room. Then the fun would begin. Part of the magic was that you never knew who the storyteller might be. Whoever felt inspired that night would shout out "Krik!" and the audience would respond "Krak!" This call and answer would continue until the storyteller felt the audience was properly prepared to receive the story. Then the night would be lost as we took turns telling our fairy tales, always about good and evil, and though sometimes the stories started a little scary, the ending was always soothing. I would go to bed feeling fuzzy and warm, believing the stories were true.

Maybe they were designed to be comforting, to teach about the better part of human nature; or maybe those gatherings were a way of keeping us safely present in the living room in the warm yellow glow of the glass kerosene lamp. Outside it was pitch dark, a dark you only saw in the countryside, with its sparse population and fewer houses. We did not go out at night, there or in the city.

According to our elders, daylight was a time for human beings to engage in their affairs, but nighttime was not for the living, or something bad could happen, and it would be your fault. You might have a chance encounter with the unseen spiritual world, including sorcerers or flying people in the form of fireflies, and if you were really unlucky, you would see scary things that only come out at night, when the dead people wake to walk about the town—or so we were told.

One of the most enduring superstitions that no one will ever be able to strip away from Haitian consciousness is that Haitians can raise people from the dead. Supposedly, one can be killed by a voodoo practitioner, but although the person is seemingly dead, lying in the coffin and not breathing, that person is really sleeping. Whoever killed them can come in the middle of night, perform a ritual, and raise the dead person from the coffin, turning them into a zombie. But they must be raised within twenty-four hours of the burial; otherwise, they will be dead forever.

Haitian zombies are not quite like the zombies you see on American television. Our zombies were a phenomenon unique to Haiti, supposedly raised from the dead to become servants of their owners, performing household chores and farm work or whatever labor the owner of the zombie wanted them to do. Sometimes, zombies acted as invisible protections for land and property. As a child, I heard adults describing how they had seen pale-skinned zombies walking with their heads down, talking in a nasal voice. I even heard that some of the big, multicolored, traveling Haitian buses had two or three zombies stashed inside to protect them against bad spells, which could come in the form of accidents.

If family members believed that their loved one had been killed by voodoo, they would use a knife or some sharp object to stab the dead person when they were bathing the remains. This was their way of making sure the person really was dead and could not be raised after burial.

One of the most enduring and frightening of the zombie legends was that zombies might be turned into *anything* the owner wanted them to be, including cows. After that, the owner would kill the cow to sell the beef at the open market. I heard the adults talking all the time about how they had seen gold teeth in the beef—proof of its origins. Another way you could tell that the meat you bought at the market was not genuine beef, they said, was that during the cooking process, even if the pot was covered, the meat would jump out of the boiling water onto the floor. That was a sign that it was not good meat, but a human being that had been turned into a cow.

Most of the time the living do not see zombies, but legend has it zombies see everything in the seen and the unseen world, an ability I always envied growing up—that, and the ability to be at any place at any time, because depending on what their owners wanted, zombies could be omnipresent. If the zombie's owner died, people said the zombies would make their way back to the voodoo priest who had raised them.

One of the biggest voodoo scandals in Haiti happened when I was ten or eleven years old. A powerful voodoo priest, a houngan, died in the south, and people said the thousands of zombies he had been holding got loose and wandered around the countryside. But it wasn't just idle rumor. I remember hearing radio stations all over the country calling people to come get their loved ones, which was shocking because many families were learning for the first time that their loved ones had not stayed buried. The gossip that week was about how you never could tell who might be practicing voodoo. You may have thought your good, upstanding neighbors looked as if they could not hurt a fly, yet rumor had it they were involved in the zombification of people. Those rumors spread like flames. They had no fire, however, because no one could ever prove those people owned zombies and no one came forward to admit it. Although the zombies were supposed to be walking all over the country, no one ever said whether the owners went to get their zombies or if the zombies were put to sleep and were really dead this time. In fact, we never heard any follow-up, but like so many things in Haitian life, that story was seared into the national consciousness as eternal, legendary truth.

There were smaller scandals too, or maybe some of these stories were fueled by gossip or envy. One prevalent superstition is that people who come into money must have made a contract with the devil, requiring them to make sacrifices in the form of zombies. The way the legend goes is that during colonial times, White planters who owned slaves amassed vast quantities of wealth, including gold. During the Haitian revolution, when the Whites were fleeing from sure death and the destruction of their property, they had the slaves gather some of the biggest clay jars, which were taller than the average person, and put all the gold and money in the jars. Then they ordered the slaves to dig big pits to hide the treasure. After the slaves finished putting all the jars in the big hole so that no one would ever find the gold, the White planters pushed the slaves into the hole, burying them with the gold.

Those buried slaves, then, became the guardians of the treasure, like gatekeepers, and the soil is populated with those hidden jars of gold. Now, if you become possessed by a voodoo god during a trance or while asleep, the devil might come to offer you a contract. You will receive those jars of gold and money, but you must serve the devil for the rest of your life, and often you have to sacrifice a couple of your family members to the devil in return. I don't know if that is how the richest landowners in town came into their wealth, but I always heard people gossiping that this is how so-and-so became rich, by sacrificing a family member, even their own children, to the devil.

In Haiti, everything that encompasses space and time, animate and inanimate objects, possesses a spirit, whether good or evil.

One story that always stuck in my mind is about a Baptist pastor named Honore. One day Pastor Honore was invited to the beautiful farm of one of his church members. While they were taking a nice stroll around the farm, the pastor saw a coconut he wanted. He asked the church member if he could go up to the tree and take it, and the church member agreed. But as soon as the pastor touched the coconut, it became glued to the palm of his hand, scaring the daylights out of him. Pastor Honore left the farm as soon as the church member unglued the coconut from his hand. And after that episode, the church member's reputation was sealed as someone not to be messed with and the church board did not call him before the committee.

It's ironic that this story is about a church member and a Baptist pastor because my own family, being staunch Baptists, did not allow any talk about superstition in our daily conversation. I suspect all of us Haitians—pagans, Catholics, Protestants, voodoo practitioners—believe these legends to some extent, even though Christians would swear with their lives that they don't. In the case of Catholic Haitians, things get very confused because in Haiti, Catholicism and voodoo simply do not exist without each other.

When it comes to superstition, there is a very blurry line between reality and what people believe to be real. Sometimes, the more superstitious you are, the more credibility you have among your peers. As for me, I am still waiting for the day when someone can prove to me that people really fly, like the legends say, or that the secret sorcery societies exist, with their beautiful magical buses that roam the city at night to entrap people who are not paying attention.

Even as a child, I wanted to know concrete answers. How? Why? What do you mean Haitians can fly—like an airplane, a bird, or a helicopter? What about the wings? How is the flight powered? Where is the engine? How do people escape the force of gravity that Newtonian physics says is not possible? My biggest question was why, if magic and voodoo were so powerful, did Haitian society have so much misery? As a child, I did not know how bad the poverty was in Haiti. The misery I was most concerned about was the Haitian men's soccer team being beaten by all the small Caribbean and Latin American countries.

Every game Haiti played ended as a crushing letdown for us kids, and the adults, too. The players were heroes in our eyes, a source of national pride, yet collectively they could never manage to perform the way we hoped. This despite the powerful magic ability we supposedly had in Haiti. Even so, voodoo was part of soccer mythology too. I remember hearing about professional players who did not want other players to take their place, so they went to the voodoo priest and caused the targeted players' feet to not fit into their soccer shoes when game time approached. I have also witnessed team ceremonies involving drinking water that supposedly had something supernatural in it, so that they could win. I never saw it produce the results I wanted, though, so I remained insistent as a child: until society showed me the power of voodoo could easily win soccer matches for us, I would hold out on believing.

Still, some superstitions are so deeply ingrained they have become second nature for me. When I was growing up, children in Haiti would not go to sleep without covering their heads with a sheet, for fear that a zombie might appear inside the room. Even now, I cannot fall asleep unless my head is totally covered, leaving only a little opening to breathe through. And if I experience hypnogogic hallucinations, a natural phenomenon where you feel wide awake but cannot move or speak, my first thought is that there is a zombie inside my room—though I am light-years distant from my childhood and a thousand miles away from Haiti.

Although I am a skeptic by nature, I am also Haitian, and lately I have come to accept that I have to hold space for all that I am, and all that I am must coexist peacefully. I am a behavioral cognitive neuroscientist and a Christian, and yet I am of Haitian descent. Superstition is in my genes.

# 7

# DID VOODOO KILL
# MY FATHER?

While I can explain away many things as an educated man, I cannot quite come to terms with the dream my mother had when I was eight years old—as my father lay dying.

One early morning, as the sun was rising on the Atlantic Ocean and the salty breeze was making its presence known, Aunt Sissie, my dad's cousin, showed up unannounced to our house with my dad's treasured black briefcase. This is where he kept all his important papers, including the deeds for the land he loved so much. The briefcase did not go anywhere without my dad unless he was incapacitated, and in this case, we found out soon that he was.

About two weeks earlier, my family had come back from spending one of our best summer vacations at Dad's ancestral home, the place where he had resided most of his life. As usual, my mother and siblings and I had returned to the city for school, while my dad stayed behind to work the land.

Aunt Sissie lived in the countryside too. She had taken care of my dad's lands and other business affairs when he was in the Bahamas, and my dad trusted her completely. She was a tall, slender woman with a graceful walk and a soft speaking voice, and her narrow facial lines showed years of wisdom. That day, she entered our home like a long silent white shadow, looking sad and concerned. Aunt Sissie was always reserved, but I had never seen her look like this.

My mom knew right away that something terrible had happened. The week before, she had dreamt that she and my dad were ballroom dancing and were the only ones in the middle of the circle surrounded by people. My dad abruptly left her alone in the middle of the dance floor, and as he was walking away, she spoke out loud to him.

"Oh, Joe," she said, using my dad's nickname, "how can you leave me in the middle of the floor by myself with all these children?"

At that time, there were five of us siblings, ranging from six months to nine years old.

My mother's dream was a defining moment for me. I heard her recounting it in the days and weeks after my dad passed away. Later this struck me as ironic, since my mother was staunchly Protestant, which meant we had become "civilized" by accepting the White missionaries' message to divorce ourselves from anything that has its roots in Africa, which means all that is traditionally Haitian. But they could not uproot everything in the brains of their converts because to be Haitian is to believe in superstition—no matter who you are. Even my mother, a God-fearing, churchgoing Protestant who did not want to have anything to do with voodoo, readily accepted the Haitian tales of superstition as if they were intricate realities.

In Haitian society, regardless of your beliefs, dreams are very much part of your waking life. When I heard my mother telling family and friends that she knew my dad was going to die a couple of weeks before it happened, I did not find it strange. In some ways, it was reassuring, maybe as a means of making sense of what had happened to our family, or of assuring myself that my world was not being upended and there was still order. Even today, with my scientific background, I have left room for this dream. If nothing else, the dream is a living truth in my life because my mom said it and believed it, and if she believed it then it must have been true, since our life took such a drastic turn afterward.

Aunt Sissie related the story of my father's injury. One night my dad either worked late on the farms or went to inspect the land, hypervigilant as always, as thieves were common. Dad would often go clandestinely and watch over his lands all night like a sentinel, or he might bury a pointed spike made of wood or metal, leaving only the tips to injure unlucky would-be thieves. This was intended to deter them from coming back, not to mention alerting other criminals to stay away.

That night, my dad saw an intruder on his land; while he was running after them, he landed on one of the spikes he had planted, leaving a big gash on the sole of his foot. It rained heavily that night, and he was barefoot, as he always was in the countryside. When my dad stepped into the "civilized" world of the city, he would conform by wearing suits or shoes, but at heart he was an unadulterated Haitian from the countryside, and when he was in the place where he was most comfortable, he lived in a traditional way.

For that reason, he simply went back home to nurse the wound as if it were a minor scratch, treating it with whatever folk remedies were available. Unfortunately, he lived in a country with no existing health system to prevent common illnesses, and although the bacteria that causes tetanus is readily available in soil, he was not vaccinated.

About six days after the injury, my dad developed severe muscle spasms, and on the seventh day it turned to lockjaw. Once his illness worsened—with uncontrollable spasms, a stiff neck, and an inability to swallow—they took him to the hospital. That's when Aunt Sissie came.

By the time he was in the hospital, school had already started, so it was not until the weekend that we kids traveled back to the countryside to see our dad. My mother had been making the trek almost daily since Aunt Sissie's visit. My dad's condition was worse than I had thought, and maybe my mother had known, but we kids had not noticed any worries on her face all week. Once I entered his hospital room, though, and saw his body lying still, with his eyes closed and tubes running inside his mouth, I began to take in how serious it was.

At age eight I couldn't deal with seeing my dad lying there sick, unable to speak. Whenever my dad sat, which was not often because he was a busy man with a family to feed, I would jump into his lap and pester him with all kinds of questions. At some point he would try to get me off his lap with only a few words, but I would come back again and again to ask him the same questions. Sitting on his lap, I would gravitate toward the protruding thing at the front of: Sitting on his lap, I would gravitate toward the protruding thing at the front of his throat. For some reason, I was always afraid that I was going to have an Adam's apple as large as my dad's, the source of his deep baritone voice. Now that voice was silent.

That day, the foreboding and the sadness overwhelmed me. I stepped outside after having been in the room for just a few minutes. I knew I did not belong there.

I played outside the hospital that day. Sometimes, I stood at the front door, watching all the commotion and the nurses moving back and forth. I did not want to think the unthinkable—that this could be the last time I would see my dad's face. When it was getting dark and we had to say good-bye, I returned to the room. Seeing him still lying there motionless, I knew that he was not going to come out alive. I cried inconsolably and refused to leave the room. Eventually, I had to be carried out.

That was the last time I saw my dad's Adam's apple and his dark, bushy beard. Three days after we visited him, in September 1977, he passed away from the tetanus infection.

Most people in my dad's family, and possibly my mother, too, thought that my dad was killed through voodoo, but you would never be able to convince me of that. I saw him at the hospital. I saw the wound on the sole of his foot from the sharp object that led to him contracting tetanus. There was a much more practical reason for his passing than voodoo.

\* \* \*

My dad's funeral was my only experience of a traditional Haitian funeral, one without European cultural contamination. By the time I was born, my mother's side of the family had all converted to Christianity, but my dad's side, as far as I knew, still held indigenous beliefs. Daddy did not oppose us being raised Christian, but I never heard him talk about belief or faith. While I am proudly Christian, the people of the Haitian countryside seemed more authentic than the rest of us who had become "civilized." They were unadulterated by the European form of religion. That, in essence, was my father.

I have gained a great appreciation for my mother's wisdom and the way she respected my father's origins. She made sure she did everything to accommodate his siblings and extended family. I think she was acknowledging my father's family and their need for closure after his death. From hearing my mother talk about how my dad had lied to her when they first met,

I understood very early in life that he was a flawed man. But I was lucky to have seen the decency of a family man who seemed devoted to our well-being. I have kept what was best of him in my memory—his duty and dedication to his family and his lands. Perhaps my mother was doing the same.

The day of the funeral, my mother dressed in a long black robe, as was customary in Haitian society, and we walked down to the cemetery at the entrance of the city. I did not know what to expect. Most of the time when people died in Haiti, the body was prepared and put in a bed in the living room for viewing—but usually for less than twenty-four hours because the body would start decomposing in the tropical climate. Even today, though they have morgues and the embalming process is more accessible in big and small cities, for the vast population in the countryside most burials in Haiti are done quickly.

I had never been to a funeral, but I had seen many processions filing down the main street of our city toward the cemetery. Traditional Haitian burial processions always had an element of surprise, something that was fascinating to me then and still is now. Two or three people would be carrying the coffin on their head in front of the crowd, and all of a sudden, they would let go of the coffin with one hand and start walking together in a zigzag pattern from one side of the street to the other, as if they were tracing the path of a slithering snake. I always cringed at that, expecting that the coffin would hit the ground—and although I never witnessed such an accident, I have heard that it has happened. At the cemetery that day, I was afraid that my dad would be carried overhead and I would be ashamed that people would be seen dancing with his body.

To my great relief, when we arrived the coffin was already resting on top of the wall across the street from the cemetery. I am sure he was carried overhead, but if they danced with him or did the zigzag pattern, I did not see it.

I remember little of the burial amid the commotion and crying, other than that it finished almost before it started. There was an open vault that was already prepared, and people sang as they put the coffin into the earth. Song is part of Haitian burials, religious or not. In my dad's case, they chose traditional Haitian songs, since he was neither Catholic nor Protestant.

After the burial, we returned by foot to the family's ancestral home, which was less than thirty minutes from the cemetery. That trek felt like one of the longest I had ever made, even though I had done it dozens of times. It was high noon; the sun was hot, and after the burial everyone was eerily silent. The adults were mourning, but as a kid, I didn't understand the implications of death beyond the immediate loss.

Because of the distance in the hot sun, relatives or close family friends carried my younger siblings, who were under five years old. I wanted to be carried, too, but no one would do it.

*If my dad were here, someone would be carrying me*, I thought.

This was not exactly true; my dad himself would have been hard on me and would have insisted that I walk. Yet perhaps that was my first loss of innocence, my first understanding of the reality of life and death. Looking out over the valley, I was aware that something was wrong and different.

In Haiti, the passage to the afterlife is deeply connected to dead ancestors. Specific ceremonies must be performed in order for the family member to be properly accepted in the afterlife. In the African tradition for Haitians who are not Christians, they usually observe a seven-day ritual of singing hymns, eating, and praying to help the dead pass into the next world. While my mother was Protestant and didn't believe in the traditional Haitian rituals, she had grown up in the countryside herself and understood their importance to those who held them. So, although my sister and I had just started school, we stayed at our ancestral home during the week after the burial to witness these rituals.

The rituals took place at night and included singing, praying, and crying. The combined effect was confusing for a kid who knew the place only as a happy vacation home, a house where family and friends gathered on the porch each night telling stories and talking about the land and generations past. Still, when the prayers started I would sit on the floor beside my mother, trying to console her as best I knew how. I did this faithfully for six nights, but by the last night I had reached my limit. I was bored and hungry, and even a little annoyed that I still had not been able to play after six whole days of mourning. I was looking to find a way to have fun.

Traditionally, on the last night of the rituals, the family would kill some of their finest animals—cows, goats, pigs, and chickens—and prepare the best food that they could afford.

The adults would then place meat dishes and baskets piled high with plantains, yams, avocados, sweet potatoes, and candies under the draped table that served as an altar. This food was intended not for the mourners to eat but rather to feed the dearly departed on their way to the other side.

I watched closely as my family carried out this ritual. I tried to keep my eyes on the flickering candles on top of the altar, but the feast I knew was waiting *beneath* the table was too much to bear. Amid the commotion, I crawled under the table to raid the food that had been left for the dead.

*Food should be for the living, like me.*

I am sure the adults would have been terrified of what I was doing. I probably should have feared the zombies or spirits myself, but after considering that for a moment, I decided this was still our house, *my* house, and if I encountered anything under the table, we would have to go at it.

The night ended as I predicted. I had my fill of the finest food and no spirits came to take me away.

My family life was upended that week. Nevertheless, those seven days of ceremonies for the dead were powerful and comforting, a refuge created by the village in a child's mind when their world is changing.

That was the last time I set foot on that "habitation," as we say in Creole. Even decades later, I have never returned to my dad's ancestral place.

# 8

# SOMBER IN THE SUN

A few weeks after my dad died, two tall, dark young men dressed in khaki showed up at our house unannounced and took my mommy away. It must have been around three o'clock on a sunny, somber afternoon—after my dad died, everything around me was sad and somber, no matter how bright the sun was shining.

One custom in Haitian society is that after the death of a loved one, the women who are next of kin wear black for an extended period of time. The closer you are to the deceased, the longer you dress in a sad black dress, so that everywhere you go people know you are a widow. No one ever said it like that, but that is what it is. I wish it could also be a way of encouraging people to look after the widow, who seems to always have small children trailing behind her. My mother had five small mouths to feed and the source of their bread had just been cut down. I can only imagine how vulnerable and helpless she must have felt.

When the soldiers showed up to our house, we had just finished having dinner.

"Are you Ms. Joe?" the men said.

My mom nodded. "Why are you looking for me?"

"Commandant Gelin needs you to come to the *caserne*"—barracks—"to talk to him."

Commandant Gelin was the mild-mannered commandant of the Haitian Army in our city. In fact, the soldiers were stationed right next to my beautiful elementary school, which had a huge white wall separating the school from the barracks.

I remember that afternoon as vividly as if it happened today. When my dad died, my whole emotional world became centered on my mother. When she was taken away, my world stopped existing. The soldiers brought her to the barracks, and even though they assured her that it was nothing bad, I did not know if she was coming back. In Haiti, under the Duvalier dictatorship, my family and most of what I thought of as the Haitian middle class did not want to have anything to do with soldiers or Duvalier's henchmen. If you wanted to live a decent and peaceful life, you stayed out of any government institutions, including the courthouse, because there were hundreds if not thousands of families with loved ones who disappeared overnight and were never heard from again. Sometimes it was a neighbor with a personal grudge who reported that a family had a member with intentions to overthrow the government.

Often the accused family never knew of any of this until henchmen showed up at their doorstep in the middle of the night to take their loved one into eternal custody.

My mother told us later that when she arrived at the barracks, Commandant Gelin did not want to explain to her why she had been summoned. She was told to take off her shoes, earrings, and belt and was put in a holding cell. When my uncle went to the barracks to find out what was happening, he learned that my dad's former mistress had complained about my mother and bribed the authorities to scare her into leaving all my dad's lands and wealth for the mistress instead. This plan worked, but the mistress needn't have gone to such trouble. My mother was already planning to leave everything because she was not interested in the kind of infighting, sometimes bloody, that comes when in-laws argue over the wealth of the deceased. Plus, I think my mother was convinced that someone had used voodoo to kill my dad and she was afraid we would suffer the same fate. Either way, she came back to us but left everything my dad owned, which meant that in a span of a few weeks we had become not only fatherless but also destitute.

In no time, my mother was struggling to feed us. There were a few days where we went to bed without any food, and everything around our house was sadder than before, especially my mother. I can't imagine what it was like for her to try to fall asleep at night, thinking about what the future might hold for her family. Our extended family and neighbors came to her support and paid more careful attention to her needs, and in that sense the community did the best they could to look after us. But we lived in a society without any real safety net for the weak and the vulnerable. In cases like ours, the community can only do so much.

Our worst days came when my mother tried to update her passport so she could go back to the Bahamas to find work. She would take my youngest brother, Luckson, who was about six months old, to the capital of Port-au-Prince, which was jokingly called Haiti because that is where all official business got done. If you did not go to Port-au-Prince to get a passport, you would never receive one. My mother left her older children with her best friends to watch over us during the day, and she spent two weeks in the capital trying to get her passport and photos to leave the country. The days were lonely, though we had good neighbors caring for us then. The nights, when we slept by ourselves, were the loneliest and longest I can remember.

Although the death of my father was catastrophic for my family, it could have been much worse if I had not had such a nurturing community who protected and buffered us in our most vulnerable time. Even later, when my mother felt that she had no choice but to leave us behind to go to the Bahamas and later to America in hopes of giving us a better future, our lives stayed much the same, mostly due to the gentle, loving group of people around us, especially my mother's family.

From the very first time I set foot in Haiti, it was like I had three houses where I belonged: mine, my Auntie Ann's, and especially my Auntie Beth's. They were my mother's sisters and we formed a close-knit group. We kids were in and out of each other's houses daily, whether my mom was home or in Port-au-Prince taking care of things so she could leave for the Bahamas.

My uncle Franck, who had married my mother's youngest sister, Beth, became a very good family friend as early as our years in the Bahamas; he lived in the same neighborhood as my family in Nassau and returned to Haiti around the same time as my parents. During my childhood he went into the coffee business, buying raw coffee from the peasants in the countryside, drying it, bagging it, and selling it to big international coffee merchants in Port-au-Prince. Later he became a commercial bus owner and was considered well off, at least by Haitian standards. But more important for me, he was a devoted, Christian family man who could give us stronger values and a better foundation than my dad might have been able to offer had he remained alive.

And Uncle Franck did. He gave us stability too.

Shortly before my mother departed for the Bahamas, Uncle Franck and Auntie Beth took us in, all five siblings under the same roof.

From hearing our elders speak about it, we knew our mother was leaving, but in our family, the adults did not talk about details like that with their children. Nor did she sit us down to tell us that she was going away. She left without saying good-bye. Looking back now, I can't imagine what it was like for her to leave her children, not knowing when she would see them again. As for me, when I woke up and found out that she had returned to the Bahamas that morning, I wasn't upset in the way you might expect. We were in such good hands at our aunt and uncle's house, people who were like second family to us; in many ways, that day felt like just another day. I knew that my mother was going to the Bahamas, but uppermost in my mind were images not of her being gone, but of the stories I'd heard about the wealth in the Bahamas. Maybe a part of me hoped she would be sending me all kinds of goods in a few weeks, including the bicycle I had always wanted. As it turned out, she never gave in to my relentless demand for a bicycle, for fear that it would cause distractions from my schooling.

*   *   *

Other than my mother's absence, our lives changed very little after she left—it was as if we had just switched houses. I attended the same school with the same friends and played soccer with the same kids in the same neighborhood. My mom's family and friends became even closer to us. The tall white walls of my beloved school were a source of stability and happiness, partly because I loved learning, but maybe, too, because that was where I spent time playing soccer with my four best friends.

In many ways, despite not having my parents with me, I lived a happy childhood, and by my twelfth year in Haiti, I barely remembered I had been born under another summer sky. The nurturing community and the God-given hospitality of the people around us gave us the confidence to be flexible and adventurous, to feel that the earth was a playground made just for us.

Haiti was our cultural home. Having had enough time for soul searching and introspection, with all the misery and abject poverty they have been eternally subjected to, Haitians are some of the most happy-go-lucky, joyful, warm human beings in the world. For them, if you were born of Haitian parents, then you are one of them.

# 9

# PIGS, POLITICS, AND THE POPE

Resilience, perseverance, optimism, self-control, and a sense of shared values in a collective community—all are indispensable in building a foundation of emotional stability for a child to move forward into adulthood. A little child's brain must learn to feel secure in the community, because only then can the child develop the needed emotional intelligence to confidently encounter people who are different on the inside and outside.

Saint-Louis-du-Nord was the cradle of my childhood civilization. It represented a permanent, stable platform where I could grow in the confidence and hope that would later enable me to face and overcome obstacles. That little rural city of ordinary yet hospitable people defined the real meaning of "the village": it was a place where children were firmly anchored in a safe and secure environment.

Most people of the town were merchants or merchant-manufacturers, like my uncle Franck, but they did not operate alone. One of my most memorable childhood experiences was watching how well the community worked together through something Haitians call *kombit*, a form of collaborative communal gathering where neighbors help each other in the planting and harvesting of crops. In my hometown, individual families operated small front-door grocery stores in a similar collaborative way, each household selling different products so that the whole community was part of the commercial structure. My house—my uncle's household—sold sugarcane, flour, and locally made soap and pastries. We did not sell rum because we were Baptist. My classmate Jack's house, though, sold mainly Haitian rum and dried smelly herring; not many people wanted their houses to have that strong fishy smell, but Jack's parents were very well-to-do, so I guess there was nothing wrong with smelly dollars after all.

In a similar way, my uncle Franck would involve us in his trading to merchants outside our city. We all pitched in when the coffee beans arrived from the countryside, wet and fresh out of their shells. Then my uncle would task me, his son Frantz, and our cousin Zack to dry the beans on a tarp in the empty lot next to our house. At sunset, we would gather the beans for the night and lay them out again the next morning until they dried completely. Then we would fill the sacks, which my uncle would take to the capital.

I don't know if an official middle class existed in Haiti, but the people of Saint-Louis-du-Nord were self-sufficient, proud, generous folks who looked after their neighbors. These people were not only defined by their ability to afford goods, but by their values: hard work, duty, and devotion to family and friends. Those values have stayed with me over the years and have served me well.

But times change, often faster than we can detect, and we did not know at what speed or which way the wind was blowing. It is only now that I realize the implications of the Duvalier era in the lives of Haitians, especially Black Haitians like my parents and my friends' parents. The Duvalier era, which began in 1957, elicits strong, complex feelings in the Haitian psyche. François Duvalier was both a devil and a good father, hence the name "Papa Doc." He and his son, Jean-Claude, terrorized and traumatized a whole society for more than thirty years, creating almost unimaginable emotional pain, and yet prior to Papa Doc's arrival, opportunities for Black Haitians were few and far between. It was the Duvalier era that saw Black Haitians travel and study abroad and even occupy the highest offices of society.

Duvalier himself, before becoming a murderous dictator, was a nationally beloved physician who made his name by alleviating the suffering of poor Haitians all over the countryside with his expertise in the control and treatment of contagious tropical diseases such as typhus, yaws, and malaria. But more than that, he is revered by many Black Haitians because of the renewed pride he brought to the Black Haitian psyche, including opportunities that trickled down, although in microscopic drops, to folks like my parents and their friends.

Part of this stemmed from his involvement in the Black nationalist movement, which emerged during the United States' occupation of Haiti from 1915 to 1934. The movement encouraged Haitian mythology in the practice of voodoo to preserve the African traditions Haitians brought with them from Africa, something they saw as the only way to restore a people's dignity that had been defiled by European enslavement.

Children from my generation were born with a certain pride and knowledge that in some ways we were more privileged than our parents, who did not know how to read or write. Yet looking back, I am amazed how forward-thinking my father and mother were, to place their children in prestigious elementary schools even by rich countries' standards. I now realize that this sense of greater possibilities came when Blackness regained its rightful, proud seat *anba tonel la*, as we say in Creole, which means "under the tent."

Unfortunately, the hopes that the Haitian masses had in Papa Doc and the Duvalier regime quickly evaporated when he turned from a democratically elected leader into a dictator. Corruption, mismanagement, and Duvalier's preoccupation with his many enemies, seen or unseen, caused him to become paranoid that everyone was trying to overthrow him. This turned his regime into a murderous group and most people lost hope. Many went into self-exile, and the government encouraged young people to leave the country, especially the perceived troublemakers, which launched a mass exodus of Haitians for safer shores and better lives.

The transition of power to Baby Doc—Jean-Claude Duvalier—upon the death of his father in 1971, even if politically significant, did not substantively change the daily lives of the Haitian people. Papa Doc had worn a military uniform and was directly involved in the murder and torture common under his regime, while Baby Doc appeared to have traded his dad's typical uniform and machine gun for a nicely tailored Western suit. But the same old guard from the elder Duvalier's time was still the enforcement arm of the regime. Life did not improve for the people living under that regime.

I remember the city started changing with the arrival of newcomers who held different norms and values. Before, we had close neighborhood friends, but by the early 1980s the community had shifted; neighbors no longer brought food to each other's homes or cared for each other the way they once did. The talented young people in my town who had once gone to the capital to study stayed home in Saint-Louis-du-Nord. Before the economic downturn and increased governmental corruption, they would return home only during the summers, but in the early 1980s, some stayed home long after summer had passed. I suppose they saw that society could not keep up, that there was no viable future for them, no infrastructure after high school, like vocational schools. Few opportunities meant they were left with nothing to do but kill time. If the country was not going to offer them much of a future, even in the capital, their only chance to make a good life was to leave

Haiti. At first, young educated folks trickled away, leaving on visitor visas, but later they fled Haiti by any means necessary, even shabby wooden boats.

One of the saddest things I realize now is that we will never know how much the talents of the young folks living at that time could have transformed Haitian society and made life better for everyone. And there was no shortage of talent at one time. I remember when a couple of young guys got together and decided to make the first radio station in our hometown. It was crude and elementary, but that radio station was one of the world's wonders to us younger kids. But its days were numbered.

At first, the station was used mainly for happy birthday wishes and anniversaries. Then they started making commercials for big merchants in our town, and the problems began. Before the new radio station came along, we had relied on the radio in Port-de-Paix run by an entrepreneur named Tobin, who had the only radio 4VHS in the region. If you wanted publicity for your business or to announce condolences or an anniversary, you had to travel to Port-de-Paix to do business with him. The new station posed a threat to Tobin. After a few months of running commercials, the new radio station abruptly ceased to broadcast. No one talked about what happened until some few months later, when we learned Tobin had come to our town with a group of the feared Duvalier militia and ordered the station to be shut down. That was a sad moment for the young folks in our city.

With the flight of this generation, the farmers and countryside laborers, who had once sustained the city, saw a better future elsewhere too, and they sold their lands and livestock to move to the Bahamas or Miami. Perhaps the degradation of the environment contributed to their flight. As a child, I often heard the high shriek of a mother chicken announcing that her little hens were in trouble, which was how we recognized the arrival of the high-flying hawk that would swoop in to take a chicken. We would run outside, making any noise we could to scare the hawk, but half the time we would be too late because the hawk was already high in the air with its prize.

I also remember when I was about seven years old and the hawk no longer came thanks to deforestation—the disappearance of the trees where the hawk naturally nested had led to its near extinction. In fact, only thirty hawks remain on the island now, and the Peregrine Fund is attempting to save the Haitian hawk, also known as Ridgway's hawk, one of the most critically endangered raptors in the world. It is estimated that only two hundred and fifty to three hundred individuals remain in the wild.

The eradication of the Haitian pig just before I left Haiti had far-reaching consequences as well, as it upended a whole way of life. The Creole pig was called the "peasant's piggy bank" because it was the backbone of the local economy. When African swine fever hit the Dominican Republic and spread to Haiti, the Creole pig was destroyed for fear the disease would cross over to the United States and infect American livestock. Even today, most Haitians don't believe that was the real reason and many will never believe it was anything but a conspiracy. Either way, many farmers lost their livelihood because of it, and their families crowded already overflowing cities, where there were fewer and fewer opportunities. A new group took to flimsy boats, seeking a new future on the shores of Nassau and Miami.

As the situation grew worse into the late 1970s, they were followed by the exodus of the educated middle class. By the early 1990s, everyone with means and the ability to leave had done so, it seemed. This is what happens when a country has been destroyed: chaos, anarchy, mass migration, and an unending outward flow human capital and potential.

But still further change was ahead. One of the most momentous events that caused a chain reaction for Haitian society altogether was the March 9, 1983, visit of Pope John Paul II. He stood on the airport tarmac with the wretched poor masses huddled under the scorching-hot sun of Port-au-Prince and offered a challenge: "Things must change." That awakened the long-dormant revolutionary tendency of the Haitian mind.

At that time, I did not know the powerful influence that the Catholic Church had on the Haitian government through a combination of shared interests. The dictatorship needed the cooperation of the church to keep the masses peaceful; in return the government legitimized church leaders by staying out of their business. The government would not interfere with the Catholic Church's activities as long as the people did not pose a threat to the rampant corruption and lavish spending of the privileged few.

The pope's words were a catalyst that gave the Haitian people the courage to challenge the brutal Duvalier regime. Now that the people knew they had the backing of the pope, they no longer had to rely on the guidance of Haitian bishops who may have been sympathetic to the regime. Sure enough, a few months after the pope's visit, the people of Haiti began directly opposing the country's leaders, eventually leading to the fall of the Duvalier regime on February 7, 1986, after twenty-nine years of plundering the country, leaving Haiti as the poorest country in the Western Hemisphere.

The confluence of these events foretold an unstable future that adults could sense coming, and I now realize how prescient my mother and her family and friends in Haiti were, thinking of leaving the country as early as the mid-1970s. They were already experiencing the rising cost of living, and like people all over the world, their preoccupation was ensuring better opportunities for their children, wherever that might be. For my own family, the flight from Haiti took a sharp turn because of the sudden death of my dad.

It started with the departure of my mother when I was about eight years old, a few months after my dad passed. In the back of my mind, I knew my own turn was coming, especially after I heard that my mother had left for Miami three years after she landed in the Bahamas. Life was growing more expensive in Haiti, and though my uncle was doing well with his coffee business and other enterprises, he had fourteen children to provide for, his own nine and my four siblings and me. Of my siblings, I would naturally be the first to leave, as young boys were usually sent first to help their parents with the bills. I was not involved in any of these discussions, though—in Haiti, children were not consulted about their futures—and I did not expect to be. I simply hoped it would not happen.

# 10

# ONE LAST SUMMER

Often during afternoons when my friends and I were locked in a fierce soccer match, my uncle would show up. First, we heard the clinking of the mountain of keys he always carried, and then came his soft voice, saying, "Boys, stop the game."

He'd always follow that up with a reference to the Bible: "There is a time for everything."

With those words, we quickly ended our game and moved on to whatever it was he wanted us to do.

That's what it felt like leaving Haiti in the summer of 1984, just after I turned sixteen.

I had known it was coming, of course. I had stopped attending school, as my uncle did not want to pay tuition for an entire year if I would be leaving Haiti in the coming months. Still, nothing was said to me until a week before I left, and all I knew then was that I might leave sometime that month for Miami.

I did not ask for details, nor did I want to know. I was preoccupied with my friends and my soccer games, certain that this summer was going to be better than any of the wonderful summers before it. Now that I had unexpectedly been promoted to the first division of my hometown soccer team, I was ready for one of the two beautiful girls I was infatuated with to become my girlfriend. I also looked forward to spending more days with Will, exploring with abandon the rolling fields of wild sunflowers in the hills surrounding his house. To me, this was the beginning of the best part of my life, so despite my uncle's words and my own understanding of the situation, in the weeks leading up to my leaving Haiti, I hoped that it would not happen at all.

The day I left Haiti started like all unending summer days. If none of the adults had anything for me to do after breakfast, I made my way to the steep slope of Morne Jubilee, a little promontory that dominates the city right behind my house, and headed to Will's house. This trip was always an adventure, crossing fields among the wild sunflowers that populated the sunny, rolling meadows with their dense high grass and trying not to brush up against it. That grass could cut you like a sharp blade if you got too close to it.

The smell of sugarcane mixed with fresh citronella and ripe mangoes surrounded me. Sugarcane fields extended as far as I could see. The tall fields that used to cover me up as a small child still made me feel as if I were in my own secret world. In some places, the rolling sunny meadows were broken up by lush, dark canopies of green vegetation. Even as a young teenager, when I no longer believed the old legends, I always hurried as I passed those parts for fear that *simbi* or other scary things would jump out at me. I slowed down as soon as I entered the wide-open fields, exploring, looking for fallen fruit, playing with lizards, or trying to catch the elusive mourning doves that made their home on those rolling plains, nesting amid the tall grass.

When I got to Will's house, we spent the day playing soccer and looking for mangoes, just as we had for years, ever since I first came to Haiti. But sometime around midday, one of my other cousins came to get me. "It's time to go, Cholet," he said. "Your boat will arrive at the port around three o'clock."

This was sudden news, even though I knew it was coming. I didn't want to leave. I kept thinking if there was a silver lining it was that I was going to be with my mother, whom I hadn't seen in seven years, but at that time in my life I would have given anything to stay with my childhood friends. When I had left the Bahamas for Haiti, I was only four years old. At sixteen, I didn't know how to uproot myself. The idea of leaving my home, walking away from my unfinished summer paradise, was too much for me.

I told my aunt Charlie, Will's mother, that it was time for me to go. Will gave me the Spanish–English dictionary he had been holding under his arm; I don't remember his exact words, but I imagine he said something clever, like: "I am sure you will make good use of it when you get to the US."

He walked me all the way back to Morne Jubilee, almost to my house, and we stood there overlooking the city as we had done a thousand times. After a while of not saying anything, I told him that it was time for me to go. "I will write to you as soon as I get there," I said, not knowing exactly where "there" was. Then I made my way slowly down the slope to my house and he went back to his home.

In a foggy moment of confusion, I gathered my few belongings and readied myself to leave. I don't remember most of what I took with me, except the Spanish–English dictionary Will had given me. My cousins and siblings looked at me as if I were a fine box of chocolate, an important prize that was about to go to the promised land of milk and honey. Meanwhile, a knot tightened inside me, or a sense that I was dying a little more from one minute to the next. I picked up a few more clothes and took the last step from my house onto the street.

"Oh, don't take too many clothes," some of my cousins said. "You're going to Miami!"

We all knew that Miami was the land of leftovers, which ended up in Haiti and other poor countries—clothes, shoes, empty gallons of milk, even rice, which we called "Miami rice." Miami trash equaled our treasure in Haiti, our pot of gold; that was the closest we could come to smelling the land of milk and honey, where money grows on trees. In the minds of the kids at my house I didn't need to take much with me, since Miami was where you could have everything you wanted.

When Marie, a family friend and my traveling companion, arrived with her own stoic face, I tried to swallow the lump in my throat. I picked up my stuff, said good-bye to my aunt and the few kids who were at the house, and made my way to the main street, trying to hide from people who I swore were looking at me.

Other than Will, I had not told any of my closest friends that I was leaving, partly because in the midst of having my best summer I could not bear the thought of leaving them. I slowly made my way down the street on what felt like the longest walk I had ever taken. At the port, we got into a little canoe and paddled at least one hundred yards from the shoreline to where the boat was moored. As we moved away from the land, I pictured everything I loved about the twelve summers I had spent in Haiti, about the childhood I was being forced to leave behind. I had no clue what my life was going to be like, but I knew it would be better to bury the memories that were still so present and vivid. That life, like it or not, was slipping away amid an endless ocean of rolling waves. For a while, I clung to what was known and comfortable, but then the heaviness of the moment told me I better shelve these thoughts somewhere in my brain for some time much later in the future. I might need my energy to negotiate the treacherous, tricky passages I would encounter in the coming days and weeks and months.

At the time, I did not know when or if I would ever revisit those childhood memories. Some people never have that chance again, or they choose not to. Sometimes, life takes you down roads where you barely have time to take a deep breath, let alone consider old memories and experiences. Even now, decades later, as I accept and embrace what has happened throughout my life, that loss is raw, and although I have visited Haiti several times since then, I have purposely avoided visiting my hometown. I hope to unpack those memories someday and retrace the happy paths of my childhood, and perhaps even discover that those endless summers are as vivid now as they were when I lived them.

# 11

# PÈPÈ EXPRESS

I woke from a deep sleep in a frenzied panic, for a moment uncertain where I was. Cooking utensils flew across the cabin. Waves crashed over the deck and beat against the glass panel between me and the violent winds outdoors, and I half held my breath, waiting for the water to breach the cabin—surely if not this wave, then the next?

I was stuck inside a forty-foot single-engine boat in the middle of a raging tropical storm on the Atlantic Ocean on my way to America. And this was not supposed to be happening.

I reached for the plywood wall of the cabin next to my bed, straining to keep my balance, and peeked out through a small window to see what was going on outside. I had never witnessed such a force of nature. It was raining terribly hard with wind gusts of twenty knots or more, and the sky was dark gray, even though it was morning. I stared up at the tallest wave I had ever seen, close to twenty feet high and foaming angrily. The boat heaved between the waves, which loomed above us like giant, windowless skyscrapers from all sides. I was sure they would cover us and bury us in seconds.

I was surprised each time the boat crested a wave. At the very top, the engine would sputter as if it were about to cut out and die—and then I thought we might die too.

Then came the rapid descent. It happened so fast it was as if I were free falling from an elevator. I vomited every single piece of the beautiful blue mackerel we had fetched out of the sea and eaten the night before, when the ocean gave us no clue of what was to come.

We rode one wave after another, thrown from one side of the boat to the other and trying to avoid being hit by flying debris. I had never even been inside a boat before, let alone experienced this. Although I grew up just a few yards from the Atlantic coast, I never ventured farther than the shoreline. I was never a good swimmer, in part because a fear of the ocean had been ingrained in me from an early age, much like all kids in Haitian society. Parents were terrified that summer excitement would boil over and the rivers and ocean would claim some of their children, as sadly happened every summer. I was not sure in this moment if we would ever reach Miami.

When I first boarded the boat, I had noticed that it had no name. This was very *un*-Haitian because Haitians like to name things, including material possessions, perhaps a way of marking our territory in a country with scarce resources and an exploding population. Plus, Haitian life is like a rosary where each piece signifies a story and event, and most things are named by how they relate to voodoo or the "White man's God."

Even now, when I joke about almost being killed in that raging storm, I wonder if the boat's owner, who being Haitian most likely believed in voodoo, placed some kind of charm deep in the hull as a protective force. Who knows? Perhaps a couple of zombies were on board too, protecting the flimsy boat from being capsized.

At the time, it was no joke. The storm was terrifying and I in no mood to accept it. I was still angry about this trip, angry that I had to unwillingly leave my friends and my budding soccer future, and especially angry to have been forced to leave in this way.

If I had been asked how I wanted to leave Haiti, I would have given specific details: after having all the summer fun to be had, after talking to the girls with whom I was hopelessly infatuated but had never mustered the courage to tell them so, after playing all the soccer games, maybe eventually making it to the Haitian national soccer team. Maybe after these three things had been accomplished, I would have been prepared to leave for a visit abroad, but in the same manner by which I first came to Haiti—inside a nice, comfortable Pan Am jet, a little bigger than the one we'd taken to Port-au-Prince when my family moved to the island.

Instead, I was jammed inside a small *kante* boat on the raging Atlantic Ocean.

This was never my plan at all.

People like me from the middle class frowned upon taking a *kante*, as it was considered demeaning. Although at that time the so-called middle class were living in Duvalier's crumbling house, the respectable way to leave was still by airplane—not in a forty-foot wooden boat.

It has taken me a long while to reconcile myself with this part of my life. It's something I rarely allowed into my consciousness until recently, that I was also part of the Haitian exodus of "boat people," one of the simplistic names given to those riveting, gut-wrenching scenes on the news, images of poor, uneducated, dark-skinned Haitians trying to escape to America.

I recoil at the pictures of Haitian women with bloated bellies, still with their perennially colorful scarves wrapping their hair, lying on their backs with arms open as if they were ready to receive the divine milk and honey from God's country, only to drown a few yards away from the South Florida shoreline, right at the door of the "Promised Land," for which they had sold everything they owned.

Or the people who escaped one of the poorest places in the Western Hemisphere, only to become shark food when they jumped out into the sea before the coast guard could cordon them off like sardines and put them in the dreaded prison: the Krome Detention Center. Its name was legendary, and it still strikes anxiety in Haitians in Miami who have had a family member or friend, a "just come," who was caught by the authorities.

All of that was still ahead of me, however. Our boat pushed back against the angry sea, and it seemed as determined to survive as I was. As each monster wave came crashing against the front glass of the cockpit, the noise of the howling wind increased and whatever was left on the cabin floor that was not tied down rolled about, seeming to shrink the cabin space. I held tight to the framework so I would not become an uncontrollable projectile myself.

Outside was lashing rain, so hard and fast I could not have seen a thing if I tried. I held on and listened to the rattling of the metal rails circling the roof of the cabin. Empty now, these rails were used to carry empty milk jugs, old bicycles, worn-out shoes, and all kinds of trash—throwaways of American society—on the return trip to Haiti. Once there, they would flood the Haitian market with cheap, used stuff. These items were called "Pèpè," and boats like ours picked them up in Miami and brought them back to Haiti. This was after they released precious human cargo like me and before US Customs or the coast guard could check the crew's documents.

In Haiti, people who had some means did not buy used things, let alone what we called Pèpè. Giving a Haitian from the middle class something that has been used before is considered demeaning. The world of the middle class is elusive in countries like Haiti, where a majority of the population lives in abject poverty, and no one wants to belong to the poorest class because once you reach that point, you don't get out. They don't make ladders for you to climb up in our society, and no one wants to believe that the bottom is where their fate eternally lies.

As living conditions worsened in Haiti, the bargains coming from Miami became too good to resist, but you could bring the devil out in us if you had the audacity to mention that our clothes, shoes, or goods were Pèpè. No one would admit that they were a proud member of the emerging Pèpè class.

As soon as another wave crashed against the side of the window, I was not thinking about Pèpè anymore. I was certain one of these big waves was going to swallow us all and that I was surely going to die. I looked for some reassurance from the pilot and the two other seamen who were responsible for guiding the boat. If they were afraid, I could not tell because they did not show it at all. Maybe they had learned to suppress their fears and put all their focus into keeping the boat upright. I heard them talking about the water pump, that it was not working properly, and I understood that we would be in grave danger if the pump stopped altogether. If the water that normally seeped through the seams rose up around the driveshaft's port, and through the other small holes in the hull, it would fill the boat and sink us.

I bargained with God.

*If you let me live, then when I get to Miami I am going to serve you for the rest of my life.*

Of course, part of me knew that this promise was not genuine because I was never one to be very religious. My uncle was a deacon at our church and if you lived in his house you had to go to church at least on Sundays, but everyone knew that church was not my favorite pastime. It was not that I rejected God or Christianity outright; I just always felt that going to church took too much of my time when I would rather spend it playing. It was torture to spend three to four hours listening to the adults praying for God to hasten the Second Coming. I was not interested in the Second Coming. I had not had enough fun yet. But, in the middle of this monster storm, fearing that I was going to die, I did what anyone, except maybe the very brave, would do. I begged God to save me. I knew, or at least hoped, good things were waiting for me in America.

I tried to take a few steps to get a better look outside, but I was jolted backward again and again. With each step I found myself bouncing against a wooden plank of the cabin, trying to hold onto whatever I could, fearing that I was about to fall face first. I was not adept at walking inside a bouncing boat, so I decided to lie down and nurse my seasickness. My already sick stomach had been made worse by standing up and watching the dance between the roller-coaster waves and our gliding boat. I felt sluggish, too, after vomiting, and short of breath. I was helpless against the angry wrath of the ocean yet overwhelmed by adrenaline, trying to anticipate when something big was going to happen, because I could not tell from the quiet crew.

Marie, the companion to whom my uncle had entrusted me, was lying down on her back across the bunk bed, holding on to the bed with one hand and the Bible with the other, head buried and praying like my uncle. During the entire storm we did not speak to each other at all. I suppose I had resigned myself to the fact that at any moment the boat would be upended by another of the skyscraper-size waves that crashed like a never-ending row of collapsing dominoes. Then again, maybe the numbing effect of fear and anxiety protected my brain so I didn't lose it entirely.

The relentless noise of the wind, the banging of flying objects, and the crashing of the waves was deafening, and yet oddly, I felt like I was in the silent vacuum of space. I could not hear anything, even myself. I would have had to yell at the top of my lungs for Marie to hear the muffled sound of my voice. It was like an out-of-body experience, an uncertainty whether I was still alive or whether my brain was playing tricks on me, pulling me between believing that I still existed in this life and that I did not. I could feel my body pressing against the mattress, though, and if the mattress was still under me, maybe I was still here after all. Perhaps my brain shut out the terrifying sounds of the storm at that point—an attempt to maintain balance between sanity and insanity. On that day, I was suspended somewhere in between.

Throughout the worst of the raging storm, I stayed lying facedown, trying to make out the high and low revving sounds of the engine—my guide to our position. If the sound remained constant, I could tell the boat was climbing up the steep slope of the waves. I could tell when we reached the highest point of a wave, as the engine sputtered like it was skipping a beat. In the brief moment when the propeller was above the water, there was no friction between the blades and the foaming waves. Then came a second of silence, when the fear of the unknown was greatest, before another free fall began and my heart immediately jumped up into my throat. In a second, I heard the engine roaring to life again. The boat was still upright, the engines had not cut off this time, and the groaning of the engine kept hope alive.

*One more wave, one more mile, one more chance to live.* But storm or no storm, we were not going back to Haiti, at least not on this boat—that much I knew.

# 12

# REVISITING PARADISE

Nearly twenty-four hours after the storm, the turquoise Caribbean had regained its beauty, with mackerel and blue marlins jumping out of the ocean as if we should all be happy in the sun under a perfect blue sky. The sea was remarkably calm. I could barely tell if the boat was moving, and the calmer the sea, the more silent the engine became, giving no clue as to the boat's speed. Except for the sun's slow disappearance and the announcement of the bright moon, I could not tell how quickly we were moving away from Hispaniola and toward other lands and unknown worlds.

Eventually, a sense of calm came over me, a contemplative state somewhere blurry between wakefulness and absentmindedness. The air was warm again after the sudden cold that had come with the violent rain and raging sea. That and the warmth of the Caribbean Sea pushed away the terror I felt about what could have happened during the storm.

As I gazed out at the ocean where it met a dark gray sky in the distance, I could feel a vastness I had never previously known, and along with it the latent power of the ocean I had just witnessed in all its glory. I felt how small and insignificant I was, the sudden realization that all of us were at the total mercy of nature. I leaned over the hull and looked down into the ocean. I could clearly see rocks below us, and it looked like we were just a few feet from the bottom of the ocean. In reality we were in relatively deep water; that's how clear the Caribbean waters are during good weather. I kept staring into the sea, basking in its warmth, and for a time felt at one with the vast silence of the ocean.

Maybe it was because the temperature of my body was close to that of the ocean. Maybe subconsciously I knew I was made of that same energy which births the storms themselves. I had felt this same sensation when I went to lie down during the worst part of the storm, but now, on the deck, I could breathe through it, aware that I was fully alive and present, free of anxiety and the fear of impending death.

For a moment I thought about reaching down over the boat, dangling my fingers in the ocean, but then I realized I could easily topple overboard. The fear of sharks with large jaws full of teeth the size of table knives quickly extinguished those enticing thoughts.

I noticed twinkling lights bobbing on the water, starfish in beautiful bioluminescent blue, gliding past the waves the boat made as it moved on the ocean. I never knew that the water lit up at night. I had seen starfish and dying jellyfish on the beach when I hung out along the shoreline of my neighborhood, kicking the crashing waves. Sometimes I watched the fishermen pulling out nets with their daily catch, full of starfish or jellyfish dangling along the sides. But until that night, I hadn't realized that these marine creatures lit up brightly under the moon.

In that silent, solemn moment looking at the light show, it hit all of a sudden: I was not dreaming. It was real. It was not only in my mind. My body and my brain knew that I was far from home, and I was not going back anytime soon.

I wondered what Will was doing and where the guys would play soccer that day. I pictured myself with my soccer shoes over my right shoulder, tied by the shoelaces, with one shoe dangling in front of my chest as I walked with the slow, confident stroll that comes from knowing you can compete with the big boys. In order to get to the field where we played, we had to cross one family's yard before climbing a steep slope, but I always looked forward to seeing if I could glimpse the girl that all the guys, including me, were infatuated with that summer. At that time, I felt that I had an edge over the others. Not only was I a good student from the prestigious Brothers' School, but I was also a rising soccer player, a trusted left-footer, and I was fast becoming known in my hometown as one of the future stars of the team. We were about to have a picnic to celebrate the end of summer vacation.

*Stop.*

I had to move my mind somewhere else. Memories of my last days in Haiti were too vivid; I did not want to deal with the anger that came with thinking about what fun my friends were having back home and realizing that I was no longer part of it.

Just as it was getting dark, I looked to the north and saw a big, illuminated structure, and one of the crew yelled out, "Paradise Island Bridge!"

The Bahamas! I got up with excitement; we were going to encounter other human beings after what seemed like weeks, though we had been at sea for barely four days. Finally, it would not be just us and the vast ocean. As I stared at the lights that slowly revealed the huge bridge, my mind filled with melancholic, nostalgic memories of living in the Bahamas. It had lasted only a brief speck of time, but at one point this place had been my home, and by all accounts our life there was stable and happy.

What if I had not had a car accident?

What if no one had called me "Fucking Haitian!"?

What if my family had not moved back to Haiti?

What if we had stayed in the Bahamas?

Would I be leaving the Caribbean now?

My family had drastically changed since the day we left the Bahamas twelve years earlier. My dad was no longer with us. My mom had been gone now for more than seven years.

My brother and sisters were sharing a house with my aunt and uncle and nine cousins, and we had not been back to La Riviere des Nègres in years. These thoughts grew heavier as we continued our voyage, thoughts that I preferred to shove somewhere in the back of my mind.

Crossing under the bridge seemed to take an eternity. I remembered why I was here on this boat and the fact that this was not the way I would have ever wanted to leave Haiti. For a fleeting moment, I considered making a run for the shore. After all, this was my country too—I belonged here, and no one could say otherwise.

But then reality sank in. Growing up in Haiti, or for that matter, in many places, the idea of rebelling against the adults' decision was unheard of, especially if you possessed a decent, functioning mind. Besides, I was no longer fluent in English and had no close family members in the Bahamas. I would not be able to identify myself as a citizen, even if I wanted to. As far as any authorities would be concerned, I was all Haitian. I carried a Haitian passport, not the Bahamian one that was collecting dust, waiting for me at the Bahamian embassy in Port-au-Prince. Even now, it is vexing to think that my mom was forced to buy us Haitian birth certificates for twenty dollars a pop from the crooked, white-haired town notary—or else we could not go to school.

I quickly pushed these thoughts down. I guess delayed gratification had been ingrained in me because I learned early in life to separate my feelings from the task at hand. Standing on the boat, and in my emerging loneliness gazing over the vastness of the ocean, I had a sense that my present circumstances were real and they would not change. My mother had been waiting for me in America since 1980, and I knew she must have paid five thousand dollars to bring me over. That money had been put aside long ago, perhaps even in my early childhood, and certainly as I grew older after my father's death. My destination was decided for me and it was not the Bahamas.

As the Bahamas faded from my view and we made our way again into the vast ocean waters, I knew I might as well accept it: I was not going back to my games in Haiti. It was on me now to find or create my own paradise.

# 13

# WHO IS MORE AMERICAN THAN ME?

Even among the calm waters of the Atlantic Ocean, life was moving at a dizzying pace. Over the course of a few weeks, I had been plucked from my island paradise, crossed hundreds of miles of ocean, survived a wicked storm, saw my birthplace of the Bahamas, and now I was landing in Miami, in Florida, in America—stepping onto the soil that so many millions around the world have only dreamed about. This moment would be seared forever into my memory. I stepped off the boat and into a new life.

I was told that my mother was there to pick me up from the dock, but as I looked around, I did not recognize her in the crowd of people milling about. I did not recognize my own mother when she stood in front of me. Where was the vibrant woman with long black hair spilling down to her lower back? That is how I remembered my mother from when I was growing up, but the person who picked me up on the Miami dock was not her. All I saw was someone ravaged by kidney disease, which she had been suffering from for quite some time already. It had blackened her earthy skin color, and she looked vulnerable and fragile. This was a quality I had never seen or felt with my mother.

I did not know her now, and we both understood that instantly. Even now, thirty-five years later, those painful emotions are nearly too much to bear. I have avoided them since then— never spoke about them or revived those memories until now.

The most gut-wrenching moment came during the first night I spent at her apartment. I stood silently, looking for a connection, for that neurobiological attachment to the person I used to know, the woman whose lap I sat on for hours, whose robe I had held onto as she made her way around the house each day.

Nothing. I felt sad and empty and confused because I realized the truth: those connections were now gaps in my brain that might not ever anchor me to a familiar, comforting place. I asked myself what the hell I was doing there. What would become of my childhood friends? Would I ever again play soccer and search for mangoes and roam the rolling hills of Haiti's countryside? And what about the stories we told each night?

I could not imagine having anything to say, even if I were to find a new community of storytellers in Miami. I had trouble thinking of what to say to my mother. Yet I did not reveal my discomfort to her, as my situation was clear to me even as a teenager.

Among the millions of kids growing up in Haiti, I was one who would now have the chance to live out his God-given potential. So many others would not, simply because of the country in which they were born and their family's connections and ability to pay. Guilt was not hard to come by at that time, and I knew I was going to do everything in my power to show my mother I appreciated the sacrifices she had made.

\* \* \*

I had been uprooted from a good life in Haiti, and yet despite not wanting to think about what I had left behind, despite the difficulties in adjusting to a new culture, my assimilation in South Florida could have been much harder. I was pretty well grounded from the start, coming from a family who managed to give me a sense of identity and value. I was somewhat insulated from feeling the pressures of assimilation, thanks to a large South Florida Haitian community consisting mainly of my extended family. In fact, one thing I have always admired about my family is that we're a close bunch. I even know some of my fourth and fifth cousins because we all went to the same church and lived within a ten- to twenty-mile radius of each other in South Florida. The same things that grounded me during my childhood in Haiti were also evident from the time I first set foot onto the streets and sandlots of

Miami. My anchor came from family, faith, and new friends, mostly cousins and others I met in school and through playing soccer, which may still be the best way for any boy to meet new people.

But the real key to unlocking the secret to living in America was education.

My first year at Pompano Beach High School was mostly happy. Like most other immigrants from diverse countries, I was placed into the English as a Second Language program, known as ESL. All the American teachers there had a certain affinity for immigrants and foreigners of all types, but Ms. Wishinsky stood out for me: White, well mannered, patient, and totally dedicated to teaching kids who did not know English. Her lessons went beyond the basics of ESL: at the end of each class she would take a few minutes to explain to us the norms and customs of the new country. I was not surprised when I showed up more than a decade later to her classroom at Deerfield Beach High School asking her to write me a letter of good standing to bring to the immigration judge, and she remembered my name. The moment she saw me, it was like I was still one of her students.

My own philosophy, the way I think of life, was always close to the ideals upon which American society was founded— that all men are created equal and that individual liberties and rights must be protected. This was a combination of the way I was raised amid Christian values and my elementary school education. The Christian Brothers instilled in me the ideas of cultivating the life of the mind through critical thinking and the rule of law. Looking back, even when I was living in Haiti I was always as American as any native could be.

Living amid the chaos of adjusting to a whole new way of life and culture did not alter what had become a natural way of thinking for me. In fact, my intellectual development up to that point made it easier for me to assimilate into American society. Moreover, I was lucky to have cousins around my age whom I could hang out with and who could show me American culture.

Even before I spoke English well, my cousin Dan took me to the Boys and Girls Club of Pompano Beach, a place where I could feel as secure and welcome as I had in my previous life. We spent hours there playing video games or indoor soccer. With few exceptions, the staff and kids made me feel like I belonged. Although a few kids would toss out snarky comments about Haiti, overall, my peers treated each other with respect. As the days became weeks and the weeks became months, the Boys and Girls Club became my place of comfort, where kids like me played video games, soccer, and basketball with me. As my English got better and I could interact more with the kids at the Boys and Girls Club, so too my confidence grew, replacing nostalgia and loneliness. Here, at least, were others who were interested in the same things I enjoyed when I was in Haiti.

I had the local public library, too, where I spent many afternoons. In Haiti, we had no public library. I was lucky because my elementary school had a library, but only those who attended could borrow books. I always had one under my arm. In South Florida, I was delighted to find libraries open to everyone, and if I was not on a soccer field or at the Boys and Girls Club playing indoor soccer, I was next door at the library, where I would spend hours on end sitting on the floor among books. I could almost believe then that everything was going to be all right, that the world was not scary or uncertain, at least for a little while.

Between school, the club, and the library, and playing soccer in the neighborhood and competitively in high school, I was more than busy and quite content. I had cousins and other extended family to hang out with, and the church my family attended became a big part of my life, as it had been back home in Haiti.

Even better, I had the Florida sunshine and the smell and breeze of the Atlantic Ocean—such familiar sensations. If I had landed in New York, for example, it would have been quite different. Despite the large Haitian population there, I would not have had the same large space of South Florida to roam around in and play soccer year-round under the hot and humid sunny skies, like we did in Haiti. I would have missed the sunshine and the Atlantic Ocean. In fact, until I moved away for medical school and residency, especially braving the cold dark winters of Chicago, I didn't realize how much the South Florida sun reminded me of Haiti.

Some days during my South Florida years, when I wanted to remind myself that Haiti was just a stone's throw away, I would go to Pompano Beach by myself and walk as close to the ocean as possible, losing myself as I stared into the blue waters of the endless Atlantic Ocean. As time went by, distant memories naturally faded away, but I still had Caribbean sunshine, a vibrant multicultural neighborhood, and a thriving Haitian community. Here I could grow in confidence as I had as a child in Haiti, thrive and be happy. South Florida, too, is my home now. It is where my family laid down their new roots in the new land.

# 14

# A GREYHOUND HUNT FOR
# A COLLEGE EDUCATION

I woke up with the warmth of the rising sun on my face, my head leaning against the bus window kind of sideways, as if I were uncertain, not ready to face forward, not ready to look ahead to where I was going on this trip. I must have been sleeping for a while, as it was about four in the morning when my cousin took me to the Greyhound bus stop and I embarked from Pompano Beach to new territory in the north.

The air was crisp and cool inside the bus, and the silence was interrupted only by the occasional passenger coughing or shuffling a paper. The sunshine through the window made it seem for a moment that I was back in the Caribbean. Or maybe it was the palm trees, even though they were not as tall as the ones in Haiti or South Florida. Anywhere I saw palm trees made me think of being close to Haiti. Perhaps it was the architecture of the houses, which reminded me of places I had been before.

Years later, I would learn why South Carolina resembled the Caribbean to me. During the fight for Haiti's independence, many White French planters uprooted themselves with everything they owned, including their slaves, and settled in South Carolina and Louisiana, bringing their architectural style to the area. South Carolina was one of the major hubs of the slave trade, too, and most of the ships passed through there on their way to and from the Caribbean.

But I was not thinking of all that then. Rather, the smoothness of the bus ride and the comfort of the seat helped soothe the anxiety of my trip into the unknown. I got on the bus that morning with enough audacity and daring potion in my veins to protect me from the harsh realities of the way things were. This was my first venture outside the state of Florida since arriving there from Haiti three years earlier. I was bound for Elon College in North Carolina on a one-way ticket to try out for their soccer team. If I was accepted, I would receive a soccer scholarship—my ticket to a college education and therefore a better life.

Not *if* I was accepted. *When* I was accepted. This was my only thought as we approached my destination, and looking back now, I cringe and laugh at myself: how could I even think about going to college when I had just arrived in this country fresh off a wooden boat? I had no idea what to expect or what was to come. My only desires were to play soccer and continue my education, and that is what I set out to do.

Soccer had been my plan since even before I left Haiti. I had played almost twice daily since age five, but I really started getting better as I approached my eleventh birthday. My soccer dreams got a boost of confidence once I started playing with guys who were fifteen to twenty years old and I was able to hold my own; once everyone wants you on their team, you know you are on your way. When I was unexpectedly called up to play with the first division of my club team, my hopes were confirmed that I might be good enough to play soccer at the highest level if I took my training seriously. I started thinking that I would like to play with the northwest regional team, and I had my sights set even higher: after playing soccer with an interregional team, the next step was to play with the national team of Haiti.

I was devastated when just weeks after being promoted to the first division of my club, I was told that I had to leave Haiti to come to the United States. But even after I first arrived, the game helped relieve the pain of having left behind my childhood friends and soccer games. Of course, it was strange to hear my favorite game being referred to as "soccer" and not football, the only beautiful game I have loved and known. Each time I was on the pitch during those early days, I kept thinking it should be the other way around, that the game played with the ugly oblong ball should be called soccer instead of the game that relies on the feet. But even in America, soccer required a ball and eleven players, and I discovered only a few minor changes in the rules. In fact, soccer was one of the things that kept me sane during the difficult transition to American life. It made me feel like the person I had been before I left Haiti, and I was determined to keep doing it at the highest level.

The first step toward that goal was to find a college where I could play and go to school at the same time. By my senior year in high school, it was looking possible. Although my English skills were coming along slowly, I was improving, and soccer was my thing. That year I was the MVP and team captain, so although my high school team did not do well in the local tournament, I thought I had a chance to play for one of the top soccer colleges in the country. However, despite my awards, I was not recruited by any soccer colleges, and I could not afford to rent a video recorder to send out tapes of my games. That left me one final path to further my soccer career: open tryouts. Maybe if I impressed the coaches, some soccer college would give me a scholarship, allowing me to play and attend classes at the same time.

After calling dozens of universities, I got an invitation from Steve Ballard, who was coaching the soccer team at Elon College (now Elon University). Of course, he told me that it was just a tryout and that I was one of some twenty other good players hoping to earn a spot out of the five or six available to nonrecruited students. He could not guarantee anything, but the opportunity was enough for me. I was going to make sure I got one of those scholarships. I packed my bag and bought a one-way ticket, which was all I could afford anyway, and hopped on the Greyhound bus.

Those soccer tryouts were much more competitive than I had expected. While the other guys were not as technically sound as I may have been, their physical fitness made up for it. Still, after the fourth or fifth practice, I noticed that something had changed in the way the team players approached me. I realized they knew before I did—that I had made the team.

I remember standing in the shower in the dorm after one particular practice, pinching myself, trying to believe that this was really happening, that I was on an upward slope again. It felt like everything was back to normal. In Haiti I'd had opportunities to be the best that my society could have produced, but here in the United States I'd found myself in a totally different reality. Now, I was about to get a second chance.

Early the next day the coach called me to his office; sure enough, I had won a scholarship, and I needed to register for classes. Though he never discussed if mine was a full or partial scholarship, I suspect now that it was partial, since I was a late tryout who was not recruited. I can only speculate now because of what happened next.

Normally, players like me would need financial aid to cover some of the cost of attending school. The coach asked me if I had completed my student financial aid applications. I had no knowledge of the process of applying to college, so most of what the coach was asking for, which I should have done before I left Florida, I knew little about. My only plan had been to make the soccer team and go to school. I suppose I had figured the rest would fall into place.

Then he asked about my legal documents.

I had not thought about that either. I had expected my Social Security card, which my mother had paid for, would be enough. I told the coach I did not know anything about legal papers or green cards, though I kind of knew in my last year of high school that I did not have the proper legal documents to live in the United States.

What I did not understand was what it meant to be out of legal status in America, or how I could have changed any of it. From listening to adults dealing with immigration issues, I was aware that this was bigger than me or any of us, but growing up in my culture, among my family, I didn't ask a lot of questions. I trusted that my elders were doing the right thing, even when I had doubts. Subjects such as legal papers were left to the adults. I had not asked my uncle any questions before I left Haiti: "You're sending me to America, so will I be legal, able to work, go to school, and fully function in society?"

No way. I did not have a clue about any of these things; nor did I ask. I just did what I was told, knowing that my mother always had my best interests in mind.

Coach Ballard asked me who in Florida I could call to find out about my paperwork, so I gave him the number of my cousin Rose, who had been our American guide since I arrived. I hoped she could explain my situation to the coach, that I'd just come to play soccer and get a good education. I hoped that was enough.

After a few minutes talking to Rose, Coach Ballard's face became grim, and from what I could hear it seemed that I would not be able to join the team after all. I did not have the proper legal documents to even register for classes. As far as I was concerned, education was important, but I had come to Elon to play soccer first and then go to classes, so I did not understand why I would not be able to play for the team. Even when he explained everything as best he could, I was still in disbelief.

"When will you be heading home?" the coach said.

"I don't have any money to buy a ticket," I said. I had achieved my goal of making the team, and I hadn't even considered returning to Florida.

Coach Ballard finally told me that he would lend me one hundred and twenty dollars to buy the ticket, but I would need to send it back to him as soon as I could.

I took the Greyhound bus all the way back to Pompano Beach. My lifetime dream to play soccer had gone up in smoke, and my new reality was vividly playing out in front of me: I could not go to school. I could barely work, and it was becoming apparent that my situation was not normal. When I first landed in the US, I had thought I would resume living the life I'd had in Haiti, holding on to the same dreams that had been with me since I was a child. But I came to America so naïve. I'd had no idea how hard it would be to even attempt getting a crack at those dreams. Throughout the long bus ride back, I sat in a daze, unsure what my future could hold now.

# 15

## ALIEN INVADER

Whenever I hear people talking about illegal immigration or complaining about "why those illegal aliens don't get the hell out of our country," I bite my tongue and dig my toes harder into the ground. When it comes to that subject my emotions are everywhere.

On the sunny afternoon when my uncle sent me out on that rickety Haitian boat, I was a naïve kid doing what I was told. I had no idea that I was trapped in one of the biggest human trafficking schemes in all of history, one that has only become more insidious.

Illegal immigration is a billion-dollar business. In countries where corruption is rampant, unscrupulous people make money off you from the moment you go to get your passport at the embassy, where you might have to pay someone just to get a place in the long line outside the building. This is not limited to other nations, as I learned after coming here; plenty of Americans in government offices are willing to make extra cash selling driver's licenses, Social Security cards, and other forms of legal identification. I heard on multiple occasions that some people were even able to obtain a green card this way. Of course, none of my family could afford that, but plenty of people could, and even here in the United States, the immigration mafia were getting rich.

Why don't immigrants go the legal route? I have given much thought to this question. It may be difficult for Americans to understand, but in countries where corruption is pervasive, where even obtaining basic necessities requires bribes of some sort, society becomes conditioned to live that way. Coming to a country and paying corrupt government workers for the privilege of moving ahead in the immigration process—or avoiding it—is an extension of what they might expect.

Paying your way forward this way is a faster means to obtaining a better future, as they see it, one that avoids all the barriers in the system that have created a decades-long backlog. It is a joke when I hear people say you must get in the back of the line to wait your turn. People who are looking for a better way of life for themselves and their families can only wait so long, because time waits for no one; they will have grown old and gray, stiff with arthritis, before the immigration officers finally see their application, and by then it may be too late.

It is sad, but the whole system reeks of hypocrisy. It is only merit based for those few who are connected enough to jump to the front of the line. One of the main reasons some people feel they have no other option than to take the illegal route is that they realize that the immigration system has been corrupted across multiple borders, rendering it a transnational form of corruption.

There is another side, which is personal for me. People from formerly colonized countries have been conditioned to think that it is okay to violate the laws of their former colonizers, because of the way the colonizers' religion is perceived. My uncle Franck was one of the most law-abiding, saintly people I knew; he would make us put back a penny we found on the ground. Yet he and his close friends and other people of my community saw no problem with entering the US or any other country illegally or sending their children illegally, either.

It was ingrained in us Protestant Haitians to believe that God is White, or if not White, he comes closest to being White. Everything in our society comes from the White man, or everything we are proud of at least, since we have been made to feel ashamed of our own culture, traditions, clothes, and even food. From the very first European conqueror who came, that sickness has been ground into us—the belief that anything from White people must come from God. I sometimes heard my uncle and his Bible-toting contemporaries talk about how we became Black during a defining battle between Cain and Abel. As legend has it, Cain lost, and God cursed him and threw him out of the kingdom. Cain became Black and all his children were cursed.

How has this theory gained credence—that all that is Black is cursed, while all that is White is good? Imagine you are a group of people who have been living in the most abject poverty in the Americas, that your government does not give a damn about you or your children, that there is no future except for corruption, crime, and abuse, and yet you must keep hope alive because Jesus, who is God, will come to your rescue. God is White, of course, and White people are from God and therefore if the Bible says that God should be merciful, then White people should have mercy on those in need.

I remember time and time again how my uncle would stand in front of us, telling us stories and proverbs that had us rolling our eyes, and then he would pull out his wallet and show us a crisp, smelly, green American dollar:

"You see how good White people are?" he said. "They are children of God."

Then he would take off his glasses and squint, while raising the dollar in the glaring sun, making sure that we were paying attention: "You see what they put on their money? 'In God We Trust.'"

He spoke with a smile and pride that he was a Protestant, in the good company of God's White children. Of course, kids always have a good nose as a manure meter, or bullshit detector, except you could not say that out loud or you would get killed. Instead, we laughed inside at the absurdity of these poor adults. I can see how my uncle decided to put me into a forty-foot Haitian boat in the middle of hurricane season to send me without any legal papers to God's White children, because they would indeed have mercy on us, since the White God is so merciful.

I am not blaming my uncle or my mom. I would have thought the same way. Although I hated the situation and still wish I could change the decisions that were made for me at the time, I also want to be fair to those loving and generous adults who only did what they thought was best for themselves and their children. These things are universal and reach across all cultures. Parents do what they think they must for the sake of future generations. Yet at the time, I promised myself that as soon as I saw a chance to take some control over my destiny, I would seize it with both hands and never give it back.

This future seemed a long way off during the summer after I visited Elon College. I threw myself into work, trying to keep my mind off my current situation. I had to find something to do, since I was not going to school that year and did not know if I would ever go back. I needed legal papers and I did not know how I was going to get them.

My mother had recently started her own process of applying for legalization, under what was commonly called the Carter Green Card, though it was during the Reagan administration that the amnesty was finally passed by Congress. This act allowed all immigrants who entered the United States before 1982 to be legalized. My mother, who came here in 1980, automatically qualified under the law, and under another set of immigration laws applying to close family members, she could petition for her children, including me, to become legal, too.

The law required applicants to pass a physical exam that included a blood test. Unfortunately, while my mother was applying to become legal, she learned that she was HIV positive, and under the new amnesty law, anyone who was HIV positive was disqualified from becoming a legal immigrant. I could see the devastation on her face when the news came. She was convinced that she had contracted HIV while receiving blood transfusions during treatment for kidney failure in the early 1980s, before they started screening for HIV or hepatitis. I am sure she was shocked, and worst of all, we kept our shame to ourselves because being HIV positive was an even bigger taboo in the immigrant community. The truth is, it did not matter whether she contracted HIV from medical treatment or from her womanizing second husband, from whom she had separated by then. Knowing that fact would not change the result. She remained in limbo with the US government, leaving no hope of petitioning for any of her children to become legal.

At the time we received this news, I was working in a factory where we made foam for patio furniture cushions. All day in the blistering heat I manned a foam-chopping machine that was located in the attic. As the scorching sun pierced my skin, I wondered if this was the kind of back-breaking work I was going to do for the rest of my life. That thought made me jittery, because my nightmare was playing out in full view. Even in Haiti, education was the only means of upward mobility for a poor family, and that was the case here, too. I needed to find a way to get an education. But I had no papers and no chance I knew of to become legal. How else could I develop into something better? How might I get a shot at the dreams I arrived with on that rickety boat?

Once my mother knew there was nothing she could do for me, she came up with the idea to speak with our despicable landlord, the owner of the Haitian slums, the ghetto my mother had been living in since she arrived in South Florida. The apartments were run down and infested with mice and rats, and he did not bother to visit the building other than to collect his checks. Being newly arrived or uneducated, most of his tenants did not know their rights, and he took advantage of that. My mother, however, sometimes talked about him as a decent human being because he would not press her if she were one or two months behind with the rent. So, we came up with the idea to ask the landlord if he would write a letter stating that my mother had been renting from him since 1980. That part was true—my mother had been in the apartment since that year—but we hoped the landlord would not remember that I did not join my mother until 1984. We asked him to write the letter on my behalf stating that I had been living with my mother since 1980. This would allow me to apply for the amnesty, since my mother could not.

He gave me the letter the next day.

I could apply for the Reagan amnesty because I had proof I had made the cutoff date, but I was angry that this was my only choice. These were not the values I was taught, yet here was my mother telling me to lie. Still, I knew she was doing her best to look out for me, and I couldn't reject her help. I applied for the amnesty like my mother had suggested. I got all my papers, did my blood test, saved up money from various jobs I was working, and took the papers to an immigration office in Fort Lauderdale.

I woke up that morning at three o'clock, energized by the thought of being able to become legal so I could go to school and play college soccer. I had no clue what they were going to ask at the immigration office, and by the time the long line deposited me in front of the officer, I was incredibly anxious, as most of us immigrants are with anything to do with immigration, especially if we are not here legally. I wanted to hand over the application and fee and run out as fast as I came in. Instead, I sat quietly as the officer kept her eyes down and looked over my application.

After what seemed like an eternity, she glanced up from my school transcript. An uneasy feeling swept over me. Instead of spending four years in American high schools, I'd only done three years because I had already completed the equivalent of ninth grade in Haiti. When I first came to America, I sent for my high school transcript in Haiti, for which I was given a full year credit. The Haitian record stated I was there for the 1983–1984 school year, and that information appeared on my US high school transcript, too. I didn't realize this until I had already begun my application, so I whited out 1983–1984 and replaced it with 1980–1981, which would allow me to qualify under the law.

A chill came over me, as if I were standing under a cold rain. I knew she had noticed.

"Look," she said, "it seems like this record in your transcript has been tampered with. We need you to go back to the school and bring us a high school transcript without any scratches."

I was so nervous that I'm sure my facial expression gave it away, but she did not say anything else. She gave me my receipt and I was out of there in a flash. I knew I was not coming back.

After my disastrous immigration interview, I used the receipt of my application to apply for admission at Broward Community College. I had heard from others that BCC would accept just the receipt as long as you had a case pending before Immigration, the idea being that you would bring the papers later, once things were finalized. Sure enough, the receipt got me registered on legal resident status, and Admissions never asked me for anything more. When I received a scholarship to play soccer, I was set—relieved that at least for the next few years I was not going to have to deal with legal issues when it came to my education. It had been almost a year since I had come back from Elon College with no paperwork and no prospects. Now, the future I had hoped for looked possible and my dreams were back on track.

Then tragedy struck.

# 16

# OVERCOMING

My memory of my mother is split in two. I remember the fully vibrant woman of my childhood, with her long dark hair, white teeth, and girlish smile, the woman whose lap I always wanted to sit on—or even stand on her feet if she got tired of me sitting on her. Those memories of my mother ended when she left Haiti when I was eight. Then there is the mother I met again, almost like it was for the first time, when I was sixteen years old and newly landed in Miami. That woman was hard for me to recognize; the smile was gone, and her healthy color was replaced by a charcoal tint to her skin, a result of her dialysis treatment. I could see the frustration in her face from having left her home country in search of a better life for her children, only to become ill and unable to work and provide for us.

Such a difference just eight years can make. At that time, the change was hard for me to understand, but now I can only imagine what it was like for her to leave her five children, not knowing if she would ever see them again. This is a collateral catastrophe of mass migration over the past fifty to sixty years, the separation of mothers from their children. Millions of mothers from the Caribbean, Central America, Latin America, and various so-called Third World countries crossed borders and braved shark-infested seas, desperate for a better future for their families. But if they had had a choice, would they have left their children to be raised by extended family or by the streets? I know that I would have preferred to live in a hut in Haiti if I'd had the choice of keeping my parents with me.

My mother did not talk about any of this with me during our years in Miami, so I cannot do more than speculate how she must have felt. Nor did she discuss how fast her health was deteriorating, though it was right in front of us to see.

A few days after I received news of my soccer scholarship at Broward Community College, one of my cousins came to tell me—we had no phone—that the doctor wanted me to come to the hospital. My mother had checked into the hospital a few days earlier to deal with an abdominal infection, something that had become routine. But this time she had caught pneumonia, my cousin said, and had only hours to live. We rushed to the hospital, but by the time we arrived, she had already passed away.

I remember coming back to the efficiency apartment where my mother and I had been living. The place was so small that it was not meant to hold more than five people at a time, but there must have been ten to fifteen people at a time in that tiny space. Family members and friends came and went as I stood in the middle of the living room in a daze, like I was in the middle of that raging storm again, with the deafening wind howling. I checked out, in a way; I could sense the commotion around me, but at the same time it seemed very far away.

As I stood amid the chaos, one sound broke through: one of my cousins saying, "Kelly, are you going to work tonight?" That zapped me out of whatever trancelike state I was in, almost like her words were an existential threat. I didn't know how I was going to get through the next few hours, the next few days, the rest of my life.

"Yes," I said, almost surprising myself. "I am going to work."

Was my cousin shocked? Probably. But something happened that night: the moment I had dreaded for years had happened. I was totally on my own.

I remember thinking how I had long ago stopped believing in the Messiah of the Protestant God I grew up learning about, who was coming to take away all my tribulations. *Kelly, I told myself, remember you had proof at age seven that there was no Messiah coming to save you. Now it is time to save yourself.*

I have not tried to process my mother's death since that night. It is like a knotty pain constricting me from my esophagus to my gut, as though everything that is in motion stops the moment I think about it. Lately, though, her name has come up when I am talking to my brother Luckson back in Haiti.

I am aware that he did not know either of our parents—our dad died when he was about six months old, and our mother left when he was less than two—and perhaps he is seeking to reconnect in his own way, as I did during the months leading up to our mother's death.

I remember how she and I would sit on the porch of our little efficiency on warm afternoons in Pompano. I would ask her about her childhood in the countryside in Haiti, and to my surprise, she would answer my questions. I see it as a sacred privilege that she confided in me her own stories about people and places I had never had a chance to ask her about. I have found myself acting as a kind of family historian now, and that has allowed me to approach the memories of my mother again, even if I still circle around the most painful pieces.

As I have grown older and had time to reflect on her life and character, I have realized how lucky I was to have had her in my life. I know, many people talk about their parents in a positive way, but my mother was one of the most kindhearted, generous, fair-minded human beings I have ever met. I never heard her speak badly about anyone, even those who had done her wrong. Sometimes I argued that I should be told these details, and she would refuse to go further. "You do not need to know," she said.

This is what I do know: how compassionate and generous she was, almost naïve to a fault. And to honor that, I simply get up each day and live my life the best I can, remembering that anything that is good, decent, and humane in me comes mainly from her. In a way, that means she is still with me. And to me, this is a unique and sacred thing.

*   *   *

I started school as planned that fall, though those early years at BCC were rough. I had so many challenges in my nonacademic life to deal with. I knew I was not even at the bottom of society's ladder; I was lower than that, hanging on to the last rung of the ladder over a bottomless pit. During my first year I would get up at three o'clock in the morning to work my paper route, delivering the *Sun Sentinel*, the main Broward County newspaper in Coral Springs. Then I would hurry to get home by seven so I could get to my morning classes, attend class until early afternoon, and then have soccer practice or play in a game. Usually after that I would nap, then study until midnight before falling asleep to wake up at three again for work the next day.

I was homeless off and on while I was at BCC, but even if I did not have stable places to stay, there were two constants in my life, my two faithful companions: soccer and schoolbooks. The soccer field and the library were home for me. Wherever I was sleeping was just a place to sleep rather than live.

In the midst of having lost almost everything I had, I was happy in a way. I had hope for the future again, even if saving myself through education meant I would have to go into something practical like the sciences where I could find a good job right away—leaving aside the question of legal papers.

But while BCC had two-year associate degrees in science, I was already struggling to balance work, studying, and the demands of intercollegiate soccer. I did not feel that I could handle a technical associate degree at the same time, and I could not give up my soccer scholarship. After all, that was my only way of paying for school. Working the paper route barely gave me enough money to cover the basics.

Luckily for me, though it didn't feel that way at first, during my second year at BCC the soccer program and other team sports were axed due to budget constraints. The college still honored our scholarships, however, so I was able to concentrate more on studying that year with a view to moving forward. By then, I had my sights set on Florida Atlantic University; I knew the soccer coach and had several friends playing for the university.

Although I knew eventually I would have to face my immigration dilemma—FAU would only accept full paperwork rather than a receipt—for now I was doing what I wanted to do, and I was good with that. BCC did not ask me to give them further papers, so I knew I was assured of getting an associate degree in liberal arts.

I wished my parents could have been there to see me graduate—not for me, but for them. I wished that they could have witnessed their sacrifice and hard work and selfless devotion to the well-being of their children finally paying off. I was the first in my family to graduate high school, much less college. I knew I was only getting started.

# 17

# CHAK KOUKOUY KLERE POU JE OU

As a newly arrived immigrant kid, I found out early that probably half of my high school—students and staff—did not wish for me to be there. I suppose we "aliens" were seen as invaders of a country, a neighborhood, and a school, but I did not have the sophistication to understand that at the time. I had never experienced another culture within my own community. I naïvely expected that I would be in a safe school, protected by adults, as I had been in Haiti.

Even amid the tension and the occasional fights that broke out, we had some angels advocating for us foreign kids—like Mr. Reynaldo Mena, a neatly dressed, slick-haired Cuban with designer glasses. Mr. Mena always wore custom suits or guayabera shirts with cowboy boots, and he carried a long Cuban cigar in his pocket. In his classroom, where he taught us a combination of social studies and ESL, he was always comforting, understanding of what we had to adjust to because he himself, as he always told us between lessons, had started out the same as us. As a child, he was flown to Miami from Cuba with a bunch of other children and no parents. But he worked hard, stayed out of trouble, and became an American success story. Mr. Mena was always ready to listen to us vent our frustrations, and we knew that we could count on him to advocate for us because, after all, he was one of us.

I trusted him then and that trust lasted long and went deep. After my graduation from BCC, even though it had been about six years since I had seen him, he was there in the back of my mind. I thought that if anyone could help me finish my education, it would be Mr. Mena.

"Josué, how is it going?" he said—of course he remembered my name. "It has been a while."

I could tell that he knew I was not coming with good news. I told him how I had received my associate degree, but because I didn't have any legal papers, my dreams of becoming a productive citizen would not materialize. "I am afraid that I am done," I said.

I watched his pensive look behind his glasses, and he lowered his head to think. "Why don't you go down to the Broward School Board building in downtown Fort Lauderdale and ask to speak to Mr. Lozano? Tell him I sent you, so he can help you go to school."

Mr. Lozano was a slightly stooped older gentleman who wore glasses that reminded me of a college professor. He also represented my last, best hope on earth; I had to get him to help me. I introduced myself and explained my predicament. Of course, Mr. Lozano would not be able to change my immigration status, but he agreed to help me get accepted at Florida Atlantic University through a program connected with the League of United Latin American Citizens (LULAC).

In South Florida, we Haitians would joke that there are no programs for Haitians, nothing at all. But I did not care about the source of the program. All I knew was that I needed Mr. Lozano to help me get accepted to FAU so that I could finish my education.

Now, I do not blame Mr. Mena for what happened next. In fact, years later when I contacted him again, it was to thank him and to let him know how I was doing. Even Mr. Mena, I realized, did not have control of everything. If he did, he would not have sent me to Mr. Lozano.

At that point I did not have any expectation of how long it would take for any of this to happen; I was content just to be hopeful for my future. For the next six months, although it felt longer than that, I called Mr. Lozano once a week and told him I was coming to see him. Then I made the bus trip to his office to ask for an update, but each time he would merely tell me to be patient, that he was working on my case, and I would return home. Still, I did not mind making the trip—half a day of my time was nothing if it meant I could save the rest of my life.

Six months passed before things started changing. Every time I got to the office, after making the two-hour trip, his assistant told me that Mr. Lozano had just left and was not coming back. I had spoken to him an hour or two earlier, letting him know I was coming to see him. I was furious. I feared now that he had been playing me for the past six months and that he was not going to help after all but would not tell me outright. I didn't want him playing games with my future. At some point, I decided to play myself. I stopped telling him when I was coming to his office. I would just show up and hope that he would be there.

Finally he must have realized I was not going to go away, because one day he had an answer for me.

"Okay, I got you accepted at FAU," he said, and then he dropped the bomb: "I got you accepted as an international student, so now leave me alone. I am done with you."

It took me a while to understand the significance of his words. I was hoping to get accepted as an in-state resident since the tuition fee for out-of-state residents was more than double, and international students had so many additional fees that they would end up spending three to four times what in-state residents paid. But he had done what he had promised, and I could not argue with him, even if it was not exactly what I had wanted. I gathered myself and thanked him, but I could tell from his face what he was thinking: *I got you for bugging me too much, so now pay if you can.*

About a week later, I received a letter congratulating me on my acceptance to Florida Atlantic University as an incoming student. That should have been a happy moment, but I was not ready to celebrate. In fact, I kept my secret from family and friends because I didn't see how I was going to be able to afford the tuition.

\* \* \*

I spent many dreadful days scrambling to find money, any money, to pay for classes. One afternoon, I walked into the office of undergraduate studies at FAU without an appointment, and in the anxiety of the moment I felt like I had a heavy sack of rice on my chest. I stilled myself, mumbling and fumbling the papers I was carrying in my sweaty hands, and finally summoned the courage to ask the assistant about out-of-state tuition waivers, which would allow me to pay the in-state student tuition instead.

She introduced me to the director, Ms. Katie, a Black woman with beautiful charcoal skin and short hair, who was very apologetic. "I am very sorry, but the tuition waivers have been given out for this semester. I will keep you in mind, and make sure you come back at the end of this semester to remind me that you're applying for a tuition waiver next semester."

I didn't know how there would even be a next semester since I couldn't find a way to pay my tuition for the current one.

Summer 1991 was long and exhausting, spent hoping against hope that somehow I would find a way to enter FAU that fall. No luck. I quickly realized that summer and fall would come and go, and I would still be scratching my head for a solution. If I was ever going to set foot inside FAU, I needed to do something I had never thought of before, something out of the ordinary.

In Haiti we have a motto: *chak koukouy klere pou je ou*. It means that right or wrong, you are on your own if you can't feed yourself, your children, and your immediate family. It is not okay to look to others for help, or for the state to send you a lifeline to get you on your feet. If you cannot make it, you die. If you can't find your way, then that is your fate.

After seven years living in America, I was becoming more culturally American, accepting new ideas and new ways of life—learning that to aspire for a better future is not bad, even if you are not able to make your way on your own. Against all that I had known and believed before, I had begun accepting that the society I lived in now had a different concept of the common good, collective community, shared benefits, and sacrifices.

Without legal papers I could not work a good job or finance my education. I was homeless. The only way out of my situation was to find someone willing to help me, and in the United States, there is nothing shameful about seeking funds for one's education.

I read about a young Haitian doctor, Dr. Rudolph, who helped kids like me who had been brought to the US by their parents and who could not go to school because their status was illegal. I was nervous about approaching him and, truthfully, still ashamed that I was doing something that was not looked upon well in my native society. But time was running out, and I was wasting it ruminating, contemplating, while staying up at night wondering whether I should go and ask this doctor for help. Finally, I called Dr. Rudolph's office to see if I could meet him.

The next day was a blur of emotion.

"Man, you don't have to be embarrassed because you are asking for help to get an education," he said. "It is not like you are asking for money for food, and even then, you should not be embarrassed."

He told his assistant to write letters of introduction to five of his doctor friends. Then he handed me a check for a thousand dollars. I barely believed it was happening. I thanked Dr. Rudolph and left to go see the other doctors with my five letters tucked under my arm.

Two of the other doctors were able to help me financially the coming semester, and then that same week something completely unexpected arrived—a letter from the undergraduate office, notifying me that I had been awarded six credit hours in the form of in-state tuition waiver, the same waiver I had thought was no longer available. I had to come up with the other half of the money for a total of twelve credit hours, and thanks to the doctors, I had that now. I started at FAU in January 1992.

*Maybe I will make something useful of myself after all.*

By this time, memories of Haiti were resting dormant in the back of my mind. I told myself I did not need to wake them; I could not do anything about them now, and actively thinking about my friends in Haiti always brought emotional pain. Haiti was geographically close, but I could not visit because I had no legal documents and would not be able to reenter the United States once I left. I missed being near the places that even today are sacred to me. I had not been in contact with three of my childhood best friends. I could not think about the scent of mangoes in Haiti, or the Haitian air, or the soothing warmth of the Caribbean summer sun; all of that I could not get back.

But I had the next best thing. I was in South Florida, with almost the same sunny, tropical climate, and living among the Haitian community, so I could almost make believe. And when I started the following spring at FAU, it did not matter that I did not have any way of finding steady work, nor that I was still on shaky ground with my living situation, sleeping in my car or moving from living room to living room of friends' places. I was in my element, doing the things I most cherished in life: studying at one of my favorite places to hang out—the FAU library—and playing intramural soccer with new friends from all over the world. I was living the best way I knew how, day by day, full of hope that everything was going to be okay. I would worry about tomorrow when it showed up.

# 18

# WHY NOT ME?

For those of us who grew up in the tropics, the summer of 1992 started like all others, with rain, sweltering heat, and tropical storms. Then came Hurricane Andrew, one of the costliest hurricanes to hit South Florida. It nearly destroyed Dade County, including Miami and all the businesses and homes that were in its path.

My family fared better than most, especially in South Miami, where the eye of the storm made landfall. But while we survived intact, several weeks after the hurricane, when I called the doctors who had promised to help with my tuition for the fall semester, one by one they told me their clinics would be closed for several months, as they had suffered a total loss. They would not be able to help me.

Even with that grim news, I hoped that somehow another door would open. I received my tuition waiver again, which included a specific requirement. If I could not pay the other half of my tuition, I must drop my classes before the deadline or I would lose the tuition waiver and owe full tuition for the semester. I didn't withdraw. I was so sure that I would be able to find a way. But the deadline came and went, and about a week later I received a letter from the administration informing me that I owed the university the whole semester's tuition—an additional six thousand dollars.

I was back where I started, or maybe even worse. I couldn't work or apply for financial aid because I was not legal. Before I could ever resume taking classes, I had to first pay the six thousand dollars I owed *plus* the six thousand dollars I would be paying if the tuition waiver were still in place.

I called Ms. Katie to explain what had happened.

"I'm sorry, Cholet, there is nothing I can do for you at this time."

I saw my whole life passing in front of me, my present and future hopes dashed. Yet I could not bring myself to say that my chance of getting an education was done for good. I couldn't let myself—or anyone else—believe it.

For a while I faked going to school three or four days out of the week. I would pick up my book bag and head to the FAU library as if nothing had happened and I were still taking classes. I knew how precarious my living situation was, so I lowered my expectations, probably subconsciously, to protect my fragile ego. Or perhaps I kept my secret because it was too painful to share. I put one foot in front of the other, knowing that at any time things might unravel further. Yet I had learned to be hopeful: I was already at work on another plan.

One day a few weeks into the semester, in between faking going to class, I asked a family member for a ride to the Miami-Dade main library. I went straight to the front desk to ask the librarian where I could find a book listing all the foundations in the United States that gave out scholarships. I did not know for sure that such a book existed, but I was in luck. I must have spent most of the day writing down names and addresses, and once I had collected information for nearly two hundred foundations, I called my ride to come and pick me up. I wrote what I hoped was a compelling and persuasive letter to one hundred and fifty foundations that awarded scholarships or grants to students. By then I had learned to cast my net wide and long so that maybe I would catch a fish or two. All I really needed was one that could keep me going.

I started staying closer to home at my aunt's house, hoping, praying, and waiting for responses from the foundations I had written. The letters trickled in daily, and before long, I could time the arrival of the mail carrier. I had few expectations at first, knowing that being undocumented made me a long shot to receive assistance. I thought they might decide that American students in need should be considered first. That may have made some people angry, but not me. Just the idea of someone in this country giving me—an undocumented kid—a chance gave me hope for my future.

As I received more and more rejection letters, I drew hope from the fact that they had taken the time to write me back. That must mean something. I became anxious, however, as the rejections continued coming in, leaving only a few to determine my fate.

During one of those long afternoons waiting for the mail, the phone rang.

"Cholet, this is for you," my aunt said.

My family usually calls me Kelly unless someone mentions my first name, Cholet, which meant it could be someone official on the line. My heart beat wildly as I picked up the receiver.

The woman on the other line was from the United Negro College Fund.

"We're so sorry that we can't help at this time," she said. "But I wanted to take the time to call and let you know that you made an impression on us here at the foundation. We hope that you will find the funding you need for your education."

The people at this foundation were so concerned about my education that they had called me personally, even though they only knew me through my letter? Astonished, I thanked her, and though I was sad at first, in about an hour my hope was back up. That whole experience made me more determined than ever to keep searching for funding.

\* \* \*

Within a single month, I caught probably the two biggest breaks of my life. While I was receiving the rejection letters, I remembered how when I first came to the United States, lonely and missing my childhood friends, my cousin Dan had introduced me to what became a safe place throughout my teenage years, the Boys and Girls Club of Pompano Beach.

*Why hadn't I thought to look for scholarships closer to home?*

I called the main center and asked if they gave out scholarships for alumni going to college. It had been six years since I'd aged out of the Boys and Girls Club, but they informed me they did indeed fund scholarships. A few days later, I took a bus to the club in Pompano. When I finally arrived, I was thrilled to discover it was still the same staff. The director, Mr. Curtis, was a well-built man whom I remembered as always being playful while being a fair disciplinarian. Though I had not been at the club for a while, he remembered my face.

"How are you doing?"

He had the same Mr. Curtis smile. I asked him for a scholarship application, and when he gave me the package, I held it close to my body as if it were something I needed to protect with my life.

The next day, I filled out the application and wrote the best essay I could: how I would follow in the footsteps of Martin Luther King Jr., honoring his legacy with what I planned to do with my life. Once again, I scouted the mailbox for weeks. Within a month's time, I received a letter from the main office of the Boys and Girls Clubs of America and David Hughes, the executive director. I had been awarded a scholarship of two thousand five hundred dollars per year.

Then one week later, another call came out of the blue. "May I speak to Cholet?"

I immediately recognized the voice of Ms. Katie from FAU. This was a big surprise after the way our last conversation had ended.

"Cholet," she said, "I am happy to tell you that we were able to find the money for you, so the six thousand dollars is completely paid now and you can start fresh. Your tuition waiver is reinstated. Good luck! We look forward to seeing you this coming semester."

I could barely say a word. The conversation was brief but felt like an eternity. For a few moments I thought I was dreaming.

I simply said, "Thank you."

I hung up the phone and did not speak to anyone. But inside I was overjoyed in the certainty that I could finish my education and obtain my bachelor of science in chemistry, the first step in reaching the dreams I had carried with me since I was a teenager.

I received so many breaks in such a short time that it seems almost implausible now, the way everything went just right for me to get out of my situation. But I was not fatalistic before and I am not fatalistic now. Back then, I never tried to ponder it; I never said, "Why me?" when bad things happened, and when good things came to me, I never asked how long before my luck would run out. After all, why ask questions for which you will never receive an answer? I knew to bet on the unpredictability of things as well as the predictability. At some point, I suppose I learned to think like a relay runner, to just grab the baton and get my legs under me and run.

# 19

# RISKING IT ALL
# FOR A GREEN CARD

"Cholet Josué?"

I sat straight up. Dealing with Immigration was terrifying when you were undocumented, and this was a very long shot. And yet it was the only way I could think of to move forward at all.

"Is Cholet Josué here?"

I snapped to answer before losing my chance. "I am Cholet," I said.

"Then you can come with me."

I followed the woman into a small, bare room with a single table and two chairs, one for the interviewer and one for me. She opened my file, and my heart beat faster then, because I knew what my application said. I was going to have to recant the whole thing.

"Can you tell me about your involvement in the group that opposed the dictatorship in Haiti?"

I stared at the brown wall, bypassing her menacing gaze—at least it felt menacing to me because of what I thought might happen next. "I was never involved with any group opposing the government."

She raised her head and took off her glasses. "Are you the one who filled out the application?"

"Yes, I did, and I have never been involved in political activities in Haiti. I don't come from a political family and we don't get involved in politics," which was the complete opposite of what I had written on my asylum application. The interviewer looked confused, but she did not ask me the question again; nor did I receive a follow-up question as to why I wrote something to the contrary on the application, which surprised me even at the time. And yet I felt a load lifted off of my shoulders. I had hoped to extricate myself from the statements I had made earlier claiming I was fleeing political persecution.

The interviewer was speaking again: "If you are deported back to Haiti, what city would you be going back to?"

Another surprise—I had not thought of this question, but I decided to be up front about it. "We don't have anything left in Haiti," I said. "And both of my parents are deceased."

"Tell me how old you were when you came to the US. What was your schooling?"

That one I could easily answer, which I did, and after a few similar questions, she looked at me with as neutral an expression as I had ever seen. "Okay, we're finished," she said. "You can expect to hear from us by letter."

I knew what I would hear from the authorities—I had deliberately failed the interview, forced the process, gotten myself heard at last. But though I hoped it would be the beginning of the legal authorities finding out that I existed here in America, I feared it might not end the way I wanted.

*I must find a way to become a legal resident.*

When I arrived here, I tried to resume my life where I had left off in Haiti, oblivious at the time to the consequences of my being undocumented. By the time I was attending BCC, though, the implications of my legal status were clear. I was ready to live my best possible life as an educated adult. But every life decision or path I could take forward would be affected by my official (lack of) legal status.

I had learned of a law in this country saying that if minors who had been living here undocumented had no criminal record and could prove to a judge that they had been living in the country for seven consecutive years, the judge could choose to suspend their deportation. However, this only applied if they were under deportation proceedings, which I was not.

That's when I had decided to do something drastic. What was the worst that could happen? Over the course of a few years, I'd experienced the death of my mother and become homeless and unable to provide for myself. I had scrambled to get myself an education and taken every opportunity that came my way. But I was tired of living in the shadow of being undocumented. I was going to find a way, short of breaking the law, to insert myself into the legal system so a judge would be forced to decide my fate once and for all.

That would not be easy, even with a lawyer, which I knew I could not afford. My plan also came with the risk that the judge would say no. But although I did not want to leave the US, the place I had come to know as home and had adopted as my country, I could no longer suffer in legal limbo. I was willing to put my faith in the legal system and take my chances.

I'd tried this route once before. A few months after my mother died, I drove to the immigration office in Miami and told an officer that I had been living here illegally: "I am turning myself in for the immigration department to decide my fate."

The officer looked at me incredulously. No one had ever done that to him before, or if he had encountered it, it was certainly rare, and would hardly be expected from a young person who spoke fluent English and acted like an American. We looked at each other for a few seconds without speaking.

"I don't know what we can do for you," he finally said, "but you're not deportable."

This reaction surprised me and angered me at the same time. He seemed to have no way of starting the process to deport someone, as that is not how the system works, but I did not know it at the time, nor did I care. As far as I was concerned, everyone who worked for the immigration office had the power to deport immigrants or grant them leniency. No one had yet explained to me the meaning of red tape.

"Well, if I am not deportable," I said, "then I am living in this country illegally, which is not totally my fault, so what should Immigration do with me?"

My protest seemed to make him uncomfortable, caught in something he had no answer for, but he was polite, and with a sympathetic look he told me that this was not the right place for me to bring my case.

Where *was* the right place?

During my final year at BCC, I came up with a new plan. I applied for political asylum, knowing full well that my situation did not qualify. It was the only way I could think of to get my case before the immigration authorities. My family had never been involved in politics. Within the police state system of the Duvalier dictatorship, we took pride in the fact that we were not political. Nor did we have any family member, close or distant, involved in the government. I was angry to be taking this step now, because lying was against all the values I had been taught, by my family as well as by the Brothers who educated me, and it is not something I have ever been comfortable with by nature. Plus, I am never one to leave myself at the mercy of others, which lying often does. I knew, however, that I would be granted an interview to explain why I deserved asylum, and that might be my only option to get myself out of legal limbo.

Of course I failed the interview by recanting my statement. I was not eligible for asylum, but I had always known that.

The point had never been to try to win asylum, but to have my case put into deportation proceedings. And that is in fact what happened. Even then, my case had to go through several steps before I ended up before a judge who would make the final decision about my fate.

This was not a quick process. For more than five years—before, during, and after my time at FAU—I received letter after letter pertaining to my case, inviting me to apply for a work permit or contest the proceedings. Other times, the letters contained legal immigration jargon that I did not understand, but I made sure I responded to all of them as soon as I received them. I knew that I was already in trouble for applying for political asylum, so I was not about to incur any more infractions. I also hoped that returning the letters quickly would hasten the processing of my case. The letters that seemed most important, I personally delivered all the way from my home in Broward County to the immigration office in Miami.

Now, dropping by an immigration office was not how I usually preferred to spend my time. Like all immigrants, particularly undocumented immigrants, I was intimidated just by the sight of one. The people inside could arbitrarily determine whether I stayed in the United States, even on a whim, people said, though in my experience it was not quite that simple. Still, with my emotions bundled up, I would park my car, then approach the building under the scorching South Florida sun. For a while I would watch the almost permanent long lines that snaked around the huge walls of the immigration building for several blocks. I saw the sweat pouring from those tired Black faces, fearful, worried, and anxious at the thought of dealing with Immigration. I would become furious then, thinking how we immigrants were being treated, especially Black and brown people, but everyone knew that the worst treatment was reserved for poor, Black Haitians like me, my parents, and my friends.

*If I stay in this line, I will be gray and old before I end up in front of that immigration judge.*

That's the conclusion I came to one day outside the office. At that moment, I decided I was going to outplay this unjust system for once. I walked past the line and went all the way up front, where I found a security guard. I was feeling extreme disdain and anger in that moment, but I did not show it because I knew it would get me nowhere.

"Look, officer," I said, "can you please tell Ms. Valdez that I am here and that I've brought the papers she asked for?"

I could see confusion in his eyes. Obviously, no one had done this before, and he had two options. He could leave the line unattended, which would probably cause others to bypass the line while he went to ask for Ms. Valdez, or he could let me in, since I looked credible. Once we locked eyes, I got the best of him, and all he had to do was let me pass by.

I was raised to respect the law but I felt no fear, at least for that one moment. I don't like when the powerful put their feet on the necks of the powerless and voiceless, just because they can. I was sorry to bypass so many people, including many of my own, who had been standing in the wretched, hot sun for hours. But once I got inside, I felt as though I'd driven one nail into the coffin of injustice, mistreatment, and blatant racism, which Haitians had been suffering for years in South Florida.

I passed the guard and went right up to the next open window, putting on my best game face. Of course Ms. Valdez wasn't there. She didn't exist.

"How may I help you?" an officer said. She sat behind the glass, looking uninterested.

I was relieved it was a woman, as they often were less brutal than the men.

"Thank you. I received these papers from the immigration office and was hoping that my case could end up before an immigration judge, sooner rather than later, so that is why I brought them here today."

She took my papers and told me to wait for a response, so I left.

This same scene happened at least five times. I would deliver the paperwork and repeat the same act of defiance against the mistreatment of immigrants, who remained standing in the sweltering Miami heat with no shade. Whether this truly sped up my case, I do not know. But hand-delivering the letters gave me some hope that I still could control at least some portion of my destiny—something I had sworn to take back. It was a promise I'd made myself as I rode out the storm inside that wooden boat, angry my uncle had made a decision for me that could cost me my life.

Despite my most persistent efforts, it took more than five years for my deportation case to be placed before a judge. I was in my final year at BCC when I started this saga, and I waited throughout my years at FAU. Once I got over the hiccup of Hurricane Andrew and had a steady source of funding, though, I was able to compartmentalize my life into different regions of my brain. I enjoyed learning chemistry, physics, and calculus and I loved hanging out on the FAU campus, at the library, and in the twenty-four-hour student studying room. Even better, my cousin Leonie allowed me to move in with her, providing me with a stable place to live. I felt like I was thriving. I could sense my shaky status as an undocumented immigrant, but I could keep it a world away for now and concentrate on my studies.

\* \* \*

By the time a judge was assigned my case, it was 1996 and nearly twelve years had passed since I left Haiti on that flimsy wooden boat. I felt so disconnected from my past life and everything going on there, from multiple political coups to the floods ravaging communities. I could physically feel the chasm of separation that no amount of sand could fill. My past life was packed on a shelf. I could not get rid of it and did not want to, but neither could I deal with it during this time. First, I had to survive. I had to find out if I would be able to stay in the US. My fate was now in the hands of an immigration judge; in a few months he would tell me what the next phase of my life was going to be.

I could not imagine the outcome, and I was afraid to consider having to move back to Haiti. The fear of being removed from the place where I had been living for so long—uprooting myself again—had become a chronic anxiety, but one so long embedded in my brain that it had become tolerable. Where would I live if the judge decided to deport me? My family had nothing left in Haiti; the only house my mother ever had was sold to get me here, and the rest of the money had been devoted to taking care of my siblings.

I tried to avoid the what-ifs and trained myself to think as I went.

Still, I wanted to give myself the best chance to succeed. I was well aware that given an opportunity here in the United States, I could become anything I wanted. I visited my former teachers in high school and at FAU, including Dr. Snyder, one of my favorites in the chemistry department. I explained my case and asked for a letter of reference, attesting to the fact that I was a decent person in good standing despite being in illegal status. The executive director of the Boys and Girls Club, an angel of a person, Mr. Hughes, and the operational officer, Mr. Sam, decided to support me all the way to the court. Mr. Sam even agreed to come with me as a testimonial witness.

Though I had character references and paperwork, I knew my quest was monumental, way bigger than myself, and I really did not know anything about immigration law. I could not afford a lawyer either. I kept my situation a secret, partly because I was embarrassed to be living here illegally and maybe because I did not want others to know of my vulnerability. But I could use the resources available to me. Libraries had always been a source of comfort after I came here; being away from my friends in a new culture made them a real necessity. I spent countless hours in the University of Miami law library, preparing my case. The librarians there were gracious enough to take a good amount of time helping me find references and learn about the American legal system. I had never studied the system before, and now I found myself in awe of how it was set up, the way cases were written to allow people to prepare future cases. In a way I felt privileged to have a front-row seat to the process. Despite everything, I kept remembering how lucky I was to live in a society where even though I was undocumented, I could access the same resources as everyone else. It gave me hope that maybe I could finally come out of the shadow and see the sunlight and breathe the same fresh air as everyone else.

Yet as the day approached for the actual trial, the gravity of the situation emerged like a humongous whale rising from the ocean while I could only sit in a small boat and hope the turbulent waters did not destroy me. I had done enough math and had enough faith in science to understand the unpredictability of random events. I was not under any illusions that my win was a given; just because I had a bachelor's degree and had not committed any crimes did not mean the judge was going to automatically suspend my deportation. All I could do was present my case with my full humanity and hope for the best.

# 20

# THE MOTHER OF ALL TRIALS

ecause I was born in the Caribbean, the hotter it is, the happier I am. In fact, I seem to have more energy so long as the sun is not directly beating down on me. The day of my trial was hot and sunny, but my anxiety preoccupied my mind. Driving from my house to the courthouse seemed like the longest drive I had ever taken. When I stood facing the courthouse, it was as if the long shadow of the tall building itself was a direct menace to my own existence. My heart skipped beats as my legs negotiated each step to the door of the courthouse. I forced myself to breathe evenly, to act more confident than I felt.

I was all alone. I had not told any of my family, not even the family members with whom I was living at the time. In my mind, it was going to be me against the terrifying immigration system, which had been messing with my sleep for the past ten years.

I had become culturally American enough by then to know that this society is largely merit based. Given a chance, I could succeed, and that sat well with me, since I had been raised in a family that valued merit and taught me to work hard for what I wanted.

"If you don't help out then you don't deserve perks." That was the motto in our family, and I had done my best to prepare for this day. I had obtained a bachelor of science in chemistry. I had stayed out of trouble. I had gathered all the references I could. I had done everything in my power to give myself a chance in that courtroom, and despite my fear, that alone was a comfort. I was also glad to know that within the legal system, the rule of law is meant to apply to everyone equally, which gave me hope that my case would be decided on its merits and not on how the judge felt about me personally.

Once I checked myself through the metal detector, I became somber again. At that moment, I realized the next time I saw the sunlight I could be on my way to the airport being deported. I did not know what to expect, but I had enough presence of mind to know that anything could happen. I made my way to the ninth floor, where the courtroom was located, and identified myself to the clerk. At that point, there were just three of us in the courtroom: me, sitting in the front row; the clerk; and the government attorney, who barely spoke to me.

Five to seven minutes later the door opened behind me, and as I glanced back, my heart relaxed back into my chest. Mr. Sam and one of his aides had shown up to testify on my behalf. I knew he was doing me a huge favor, driving from Fort Lauderdale all the way to downtown Miami, where the proceedings were taking place. But more than anything, seeing Mr. Sam put me a little more at ease: if the judge decided to deport me, at least someone would know and be able to tell my family.

At the time, I was surprised to find the staff somewhat cold, including the government lawyer. I was anxious to talk and have someone, anyone, break the tension I was feeling. Now I realize they were there to do their job, a job that could be very uncomfortable at times, I am sure, since they had decided the fate of many illegal immigrants before my case. My nerves were wound so tight I was shaking. I had no sense of time. All I remember is that it felt like a very long time before the judge was ready, or maybe it was a very short time—I couldn't tell you now. I do remember the clerk suddenly saying, "All rise."

Then something happened I did not expect. A wheelchair rolled into the courtroom. Sitting in the wheelchair was the judge, tall and lanky with white hair; he must have been in his fifties, but he looked like he was in pain, possibly with a degenerative nerve illness.

The moment he started speaking, I could tell he had as sharp a mind as any judge. He was stern, but I sensed he was fair, that he would decide my case on its merits, as I had hoped. That made me apprehensive too. At least I knew my chances were fifty-fifty.

The clerk identified everyone present, including me, and when he acknowledged I was representing myself, the courtroom became eerily silent. It felt like someone's life was literally hanging in the balance, and in a way, mine was.

When the clerk called me up front to testify, I raised my hand and promised that I would tell the truth, the whole truth, and nothing but the truth, so help me God.

"Your Honor, all I want is a clean slate, and I am taking responsibility for having entered this country illegally."

I felt anger and relief as I told the court everything: "My driver's license was made for me with the help of a family friend. My Social Security card was paid for me by my mother."

At that moment I had no fear, knowing that whatever was going to happen was going to happen. What washed over me instead was relief—relief to finally be getting these things off my chest, because I was ashamed of them. In another way, I wanted to take a jab at the system for being corrupt. I wanted to show that I was not the only one culpable—to remind everyone inside the courtroom what they all already knew, that illegal immigration is a multibillion-dollar business that has been legitimized by people like the corrupt sheriff who sold documents to my mother, but also, if unknowingly, by good and decent people in America.

"I do not have a criminal record, Your Honor. In fact, I have never come close to doing illegal things, not even to eat or find a place to sleep, not even when I was homeless."

I was well aware there were countless easier, illegal paths that I could have taken to survive; I'd had hundreds of opportunities to screw up my life if I had wanted. One hot night, I remember, a high school friend had offered to get me in on selling drugs: "This is what you need to do to get cars, nice clothes, and girls." I shrugged him off with a gesture, not saying anything aloud, but I asked myself in front of him: how dare you? Thankfully I still had a community and close-knit family in South Florida, and there were lines we didn't cross. What might have happened if I hadn't said no?

I looked over at the government's attorney, a White woman with brunette hair, and saw her disdain for me plain on her face. That's when I became convinced that I had done the right thing by studying the law before my hearing. She seemed surprised I was better prepared than she was, even equipped with my own character witness. Perhaps she did not like that, or maybe she just did not expect it. In any case, she didn't have much to say at all, and the judge took over the case, doing most of the talking and questioning.

"When, exactly, did you get to the United States? Who did you come with? Did you know that you would not be going back?"

The questions were persistent, yet I was comforted knowing that this was not personal, that he was applying the law equally to me as he would to anyone else. I was also glad that I had a trial by a judge and not by a jury, as I felt like I could make my case better one on one.

Maybe this was wishful thinking. When the judge started asking me if I paid taxes, I was caught off guard momentarily, especially at how hard he went after me for not having filed my income tax form. "I did not know I was required to file a tax return in high school," I said. I was trying to keep my emotions in check, but I felt like a fish caught in a dragnet with no holes to escape. I'd been in the United States for years before I knew about income taxes or the need to file. My teen-age years I'd worked as a bag boy at the supermarket, making minimum wage or even less, so why was he giving me a hard time about paying taxes? I would have gotten money back had I filed a return, since my family income was below the poverty line. The courtroom was air-conditioned, but I was sweating as if I were running down the soccer field in pursuit of a goal. I'd known my chances of staying in the US were slim, but I held out hope. Now my confidence took a nosedive. Maybe I was not that knowledgeable about the law after all.

Then, something came over me. I had been watching the news about the Iran-Contra affair on television, and I had seen how Colonel Oliver North tried to wiggle his way out of handcuffs using those infamous words: "I can't recall." That infuriated the senators who were questioning him, but he continued answering like that until they stopped asking any more questions. I hoped the same methodology might work for me.

"I can't recall," I said. I decided to become lawyerly, or at least what I thought that was supposed to sound like. "I cannot recall, Your Honor, whether I filed taxes or not."

My response seemed to anger the judge, who reprimanded me in a soft but stern voice for trying to evade the answer.

I really had nothing more to say about taxes, though, and at some point the judge and the government lawyer had no more questions. Then, Mr. Sam from the Boys Club asked the judge if he could say some words on my behalf. I don't remember exactly what he said, but I do remember glancing back and forth between the judge and Mr. Sam on the witness stand, waiting for some indication from the judge that everything would be okay. When Mr. Sam finished, the courtroom was engulfed in a foreboding silence.

"Mr. Josué," said the clerk. "You will be hearing in due time from the court by mail, regarding the decision in your case. Court is adjourned."

Suddenly, everything was over. The trial of my life was finished almost as soon as it had begun, as if it were of no consequence, despite what it meant for my future here in the United States.

I was still in a trance as I took the elevator to the main floor and walked through the halls, my pace slowing as if I were trying to stretch the elastic band of time and take a peek at what my future held. But I could not catch even a glimpse. As I stepped out onto the sidewalk and turned my back to the courthouse, I could feel its long shadow pushing me into the Miami street, into the scary unknown.

# 21

# THE DECISION

Though the trial was over, I left the courthouse feeling more uncertain than ever. The entire immigration system was no longer a theory in my mind. I was in the midst of it, and it held my fate. Nevertheless, I was confident the result would be fair, regardless of the outcome. I guess that was my faith in America at work. I was aware the decision could go either way, and after the judge grilled me on the witness stand over paying taxes and applying for political asylum, I thought maybe he would not rule in my favor after all. I wished I could be a fly on the wall of his chambers, just to see if I could figure out how he was going to decide my future. I could not conjure up the inner workings of a judge's mind, and I had no reason to believe his hard questions meant he would deny my petition. Still, the fear made me edgy, and I wanted to hold on to even the smallest bit of hope.

That's exactly what I did. By the time I got in my car outside the courthouse, I felt a little lighter, as if part of the weight I had been carrying for the past twelve years had disappeared. I had not been handcuffed and handed over to be shipped off the next day to the Caribbean, a possibility I had considered because it had happened to many who came before me. No. Instead, I had thanked Mr. Sam for coming to testify on my behalf, then walked out of the building and headed home, where I would spend six months of sleepless nights waiting for the judge's decision.

If it had bothered me before that my legal status was in limbo, now it grated on me every moment of every day. I had no plans for how I would deal with rejection, when and if that time came. But knowing that I did not have any guarantee of what the decision would be, I made one last attempt to plead my case. The day after the trial, I wrote the judge the most passionate, persuasive letter I had ever attempted, begging him to let me stay in America. I described how, despite almost insurmountable obstacles, I had managed to negotiate my way through legal limbo *and* obtain a bachelor of science in chemistry. I promised that if I were given the opportunity to stay, I would do everything I could to make up for any character flaws I'd shown by lying on my asylum application.

It was a very passionate letter from a desperate young man. I mentioned my appreciation for the life I'd had so far in the United States. I told the judge I looked forward to contributing to a country that had given me a chance even when I entered it illegally. I said that my hope was to pursue a career in science and medicine, which I was leaning toward after my experience with my mother's illness. I thought I could become a good physician and give back to society by restoring the health of the sick. At the end of the letter, I promised that if I was given the opportunity to stay, I would make the best of it and never take it for granted.

"Of those to whom much is given, much is also expected."

I included this quote and signed off, praying it would make a difference. Was it enough? I didn't know. I had no idea if the judge would even get the letter, much less read it, but I was determined to give myself the best chance I could.

As the weeks of waiting accumulated, my insomnia became more pronounced. I spent nights recalling each moment of the trial in my mind, asking myself over and over what I could have done differently, or better. During the day, I became irritable and kept more to myself, although no one could have noticed.

The trial had taken place in December 1995, and as the summer of 1996 drew to a close, I knew the day had to be approaching fast when the decision would be made. Over the next several weeks I spent more time checking the mailbox than I had done while awaiting the scholarship letters from FAU.

Finally, one sweltering September day, the letter from Immigration was waiting in the mailbox. My heart skipped several beats while I held it in my shaking hand. In this envelope, the fate of my life resided, and for a while I stood there looking at it under the hot sun—more eager but more afraid than ever to finally know which direction my life was to take.

How could the balance of my entire life be contained inside an envelope?

My anxiety rushed me to open it, but even then, I did not read the letter beginning with the first page. Instead, I flipped forward to page nine. The first eight pages mostly discussed the facts of my case and other similar cases that came before mine and how the court dealt with them, but the only part I was interested in was the last paragraph of the last page.

"Based upon the above, the Court shall grant the application for suspension of deportation." I read it again, an almost out-of-body experience, like I was watching myself stand by the mailbox reading the letter. "The Court shall grant . . ." *The Court shall grant.* Then I read it aloud, as if hearing it would confirm for me that it was real.

"Based upon the above, the Court shall grant the application for suspension of deportation."

I'd done it. My unending nightmare had come to an end. I was now a legal alien, a resident of the United States of America.

Later, after I read through the entire decision, I was surprised to discover that the judge had not only received my letter but had read it and even quoted it in his decision.

". . . the Court is not treating lightly the false statements the respondent gave to the Service. As the respondent said himself in a letter to the Court, 'Those who have been given great gifts, also carry heavy burdens.' It is indeed a great gift to receive lawful permanent residency in the United States. The Court admonishes the respondent to reflect upon what he has been given, and to commit to never give false testimony or mislead our government ever again for any reason. It is ordered that the application for suspension of deportation be granted."

I put the letter back in the big white envelope. *Those who have been given great gifts, also carry heavy burdens.* In my letter to the judge I had mentioned medical school, a goal I had long had but until that day I was never sure that I could reach. I was too much of a realist—I knew the mountain I'd have to climb, that only if I could become a legal resident could I dare to dream much further than my nose. Now, I had crossed that mountain. I breathed a great sigh of relief. Then I went upstairs, put the letter in a secure place, and decided to apply to medical school.

\*   \*   \*

*Can one's life really turn so beautifully in a single day? Only in America . . .*

I still have ambivalent feelings about the way I entered this country. It has never been lost on me that the same family who raised me to respect law and order, and who had wanted me to have a better life, were willing to break the law to make that happen for me. I take comfort in knowing that even someone like me, alone on the outskirts of society, invisible and uncounted, could find a way to belong here. I'm grateful that the lawmakers of this country left provisions for people like me to find room to become productive members of society. I also take pride in the fact that my story, and the story of kids like me, can only be made in America and nowhere else, and that all of us can enter into the greatest experiment in human history.

When Emma Lazarus said, "Give me your tired, your poor, your huddled masses yearning to be free. The wretched refuse of your teeming shore," I now know that she was also talking about kids like me.

# EPILOGUE

*There was once a village where every child, whether they were born inside or outside the village, was given a tree of their own. The umbilical cord was saved and dried to be planted under a fruit tree, and if the parents died early, all the instructions that they did not have time to give their children would be in the fruits that the tree bore. The knowledge of living would be held within that fruit.*

*Now a fruit tree might grow to maturity and bear fruit seasonally, but if the tree had a child's umbilical cord planted beneath it, that tree would grow to mature height but would only produce fruit for that specific child on demand.*

*Every time the child did not know what to do or was about to make a major life decision, they would stand in front of the tree waiting for when the sun was directly overhead, and only then would they tap the tree: three times if their birth was on the third day of the week or four times if their birth fell on the fourth day of the week and so on. Then a coconut or other fruit would fall from the top of the tree, and once the child drank the water contained within the fruit, all the answers they sought would be revealed.*

Until the January 2010 earthquake in Haiti, I had given up all thoughts of my own fruit tree on my father's ancestral lands, the place where my umbilical cord is planted. I had forgotten the warm, early summer morning during what would be my last summer in the lost paradise of my boyhood, my father's family village, when I woke to find that the starry sky had already given way to the rising sun. I had forgotten the place where they buried my umbilical cord, and the smell of ripe avocadoes and mangoes and the fertile deciduous soil and half-rotten leaves, which together gave that part of Haiti its unique scent. I think I could walk into that region blindfolded and still identify it.

Perhaps that is because physically I am part of the land myself. This is the most precious gift my parents could have given me: the assurance that even if the coconut tree is long gone, my DNA remains in the soil under the sunny Caribbean sky. To me, that is everything.

But before the earthquake, all that had vanished from my mind.

The day I set foot in Miami as a teenager, my intention was simple: to pick up the pieces I had brought with me from my childhood and to assimilate and gain a foothold in the great melting pot of American society. My past was too much of a burden, a heavy load that I could not take on. But I did not expect assimilation to be so complicated. I did not know it was going to take some kind of jujitsu move for me to negotiate my way to finding a more authentic, enduring self.

The moment I learned of the earthquake, the ground shifted beneath me again, as though whatever I had built to stand on had cracked and splintered. But by then I understood that full belonging, both physically and psychologically, is much more complicated for people like me, who have lived in and become part of several cultures. In fact, the question of the authentic self is an ever-evolving and at times elusive idea to wrap myself around; whether living in America or visiting Haiti, I still experience being "the other" almost daily. Even among Bahamians, I cannot feel as though I fully belong.

So, what can I hold on to?

I know that in a physical sense I will never fully belong in any one place. I have pieces of myself in the Bahamas, in Haiti, and in South Florida. But I also know that I am not alone, even if my particular circumstances are unique. We all have a need to feel accepted, to be acknowledged, to recognize a place that we can call our own.

The technological and economic changes of the past seventy years have reduced the distance between communities, making the entire world more interconnected and more interdependent. These changes have improved the lives of billions of people by lifting them out of poverty, but at the same time those changes have had serious consequences on a more personal level. Many regions have seen the dislocation of millions, and the rapidly changing communities and social connections have given rise to a profound sense of loss for many of us who now feel displaced on a psychological level.

The glue that holds family together, and civilizations past and present, has always been the ability to pass on the values that form a blueprint for our well-being and the survival and sustainability of family and society. It is through storytelling that we share these values, these encoded instructions for future generations. Just like the coconut tree in the folktale.

Storytelling is where it begins, but I am far from ready to say the tale is ended or that I have discovered all the answers I need to move forward with my life. I realize now that part of what I experienced the day of the earthquake was the call to continue my own story, the story that began many generations before me in all the nations that have formed part of my identity. And though I have reached into my own distant past to build a new, stable platform for myself, writing this book was just the beginning. I must return to my own coconut tree for the answers I may find there. I need to travel to the places where I have lived, to gain a deeper understanding of how I got here, and to more fully decode the values that have been handed down to me by those who have come before.

I invite you, the reader, to go with me in this next stage of the journey. Together, let's travel back to the fruit trees of the past, to connect with the people and places that form part of our individual and collective identity. And as we build our own stable platform for the next step in our own lives, perhaps we can bring that same stability to the whole community in a constantly changing world.

# ACKNOWLEDGMENTS

To my mother, Immacula Frederick, my alpha and my omega: I exist because you brought me into this world. In a metaphysical way, I cannot miss you, because you have always been with me, a constant guiding light and the source of everything that is good in me, if indeed I have any compassion, emotional intelligence, and humanity. You are my hero and my saint, and I have tried to be a decent human being because I came from you.

\* \* \*

To the women in my family on my mother's side: Thank you for the sacrifices you made at the cost of forgetting yourselves, just to give a better future to the next generation. The sacrifices made by women all over the world for their children's sake are godlike.

\* \* \*

Christina M. Frey (Page Two Editorial): Until I met you, this book project was just a dream. I had gone through several editors and was struggling like hell; I had not known how excruciating it was going to be to attempt to write a manuscript. As my writing coach, you held my hand the whole way, guiding me through outlining and book development, and sometimes, like I'd often joke, acting as my therapist. I know now what the best in the editing profession looks like. Thank you for your advice, your patience, and the way you were always there to listen on days I did not feel like doing this writing thing. Without you, this book would not exist.

Stephanie Chandler (Nonfiction Authors Association): You are one of the most generous people I know in the writing community. I remember the first time I called you about five years ago with my big idea of becoming a writer. Unlike most people, who looked at me like I had truly lost it, you took time out of your busy schedule to talk to me for over an hour about my plans for the book. I am forever grateful that you have been part of my supportive writing community.

David Tabatsky, my substantive editor: Thank you for understanding so well the deeper meaning behind my writing. You are a rare combination of genius and good-naturedness, and one of the most caring, wisest men I have met. Thank you for working with me and for taking the time to listen.

Katherine Pickett (POP Editing), my line editor and copyeditor: From the moment I first spoke with you, I felt assured you would treat my writing with the same care and respect that you would give your own. Thank you for your thorough work and for your thoughtful, respectful queries. I knew throughout the editing process that I was in the best of hands.

Melissa Wuske, my content editor: I am grateful for your knowledge, expertise, and professionalism, particularly in the way you made sure you answered all of my questions after I got the manuscript back. Your comments and responses made it a positive experience, and my book is the better for it.

Rachel Lee Cherry, my proofreader: Thank you for giving such attention to detail in this final phase. I am grateful for your eagle eye!

# TO THE BOYS AND GIRLS CLUBS OF AMERICA

When I was shipped to Miami, South Florida, to join my mother here, I did not know how traumatic it would be until I was living it. How could I have truly understood what it meant to leave my childhood friends, my village, and all the things that made me feel good about myself? Here I didn't have my soccer games or my mangoes. I'd lost the community that had been central to my well-being as a child.

I will always be grateful I tagged along with my cousin Dan to the Boys and Girls Club one day, because that is where I rediscovered community. In a very real way, the local Boys and Girls Club became my safe sanctuary in a scary world. And later on, years after I aged out of the Boys and Girls Club, it came to my rescue when I could not afford my university tuition by giving me a scholarship to attend Florida Atlantic University.

Now it is my turn to give back. A portion of book sales will be donated to the Boys and Girls Club of Broward County, Florida, which made such a difference in my life. Each purchase helps kids who are seeking a safe place where they can grow in confidence and find community.

# ABOUT THE AUTHOR

## Cholet Kelly Josué, MD

Cholet Kelly Josué is a Bahamian-born Haitian American author and physician seeking a home among the three cultures that have played a role in his life. Born in the Bahamas of Haitian parents who wanted their children to experience their ancestral roots, Cholet moved to Haiti with his siblings when he was four years old. There he spent the next twelve years of his life reveling in a simple and decent, if checkered, childhood until he was sent across the Caribbean Sea in a wooden boat to join his mother in South Florida after the death of his father.

While still an undocumented immigrant, Cholet earned a bachelor of science degree in chemistry from Florida Atlantic University. Then he spent the next six months at the University of Miami law library preparing to represent himself in the trial of his life: the quest to become a legal resident.

Cholet received his medical degree from Morehouse School of Medicine in Atlanta and did his residency at the University of Illinois at Chicago. He practices medicine in Maryland with a functional and integrative approach and draws on his special interest in behavioral neurology and neuropsychiatry.

# THE NEXT STEP

When I finished revising this book, I realized my writing journey had only just begun. Now I must return to the many places where I grew up and matured—Nassau, Bahamas; Saint-Louis-du-Nord, Haiti; and Miami, South Florida—and put the pieces back together in order to gain a deeper understanding of those places, the lands, and the people. Only then can I create a stable platform on which to build the next chapter of my life.

I invite you to join me on my quest so we can share and have conversation along the journey. Visit www.drjosue.com, and click "Join my tribe" for updates, blog access, and news about future book projects.

CPSIA information can be obtained
at www.ICGtesting.com
Printed in the USA
FFHW011929040619
52835914-58371FF